TEACHER'S PET PUBLICATIONS

PUZZLE PACK for
The Light in the Forest

based on the book by
Conrad Richter

Written by
William T. Collins

© 2005 Teacher's Pet Publications
All Rights Reserved

The materials in this packet are copyrighted
by Teacher's Pet Publications, Inc.

These pages may be duplicated by the purchaser
for use in the purchaser's own classroom.

Copying any of these materials and distributing them
for any other purpose is a violation of the copyright laws.

© 2005 Teacher's Pet Publications, Inc.
www.tpet.com

INTRODUCTION

If you already own the LitPlan for this title, this Puzzle Pack will refresh your Unit Resource Materials and Vocabulary Resource Materials sections plus give you additional materials you can substitute into the tests. If you do not already have a complete LitPlan, these pages will give you some supplemental materials to use with your own plan. There are two main groups of materials: one set for unit words (such as characters' names, symbols, places, etc.) and one set for vocabulary words associated with the book.

WORD LIST

There is a word list for both the unit words and the vocabulary words. These lists show you which words are being used in the materials and the clues or definitions being used for those words. You may want to give students a word list with clues/definitions to help them, or you may want students to only have a word list (without clues/definitions) if you want them to work a little harder. Both are available for duplication. The word lists can also be your "calling key" for the bingo games.

FILL IN THE BLANK AND MATCHING

There are 4 each of the fill in the blank and matching worksheets for both the unit and vocabulary words. These pages can be used either as extra worksheets for students or as objective parts of a unit test. They can be done individually if students need extra help or as a whole class activity to review the material covered.

MAGIC SQUARES

The magic squares not only reinforce the material covered but also work on reasoning and math skills. Many teachers have told us that their students really enjoy doing these!

WORD SEARCH PUZZLES

The word search words go in all directions, as indicated on your answer keys. Two of the word search puzzles have the clues listed rather than the words. This makes the puzzle a little more difficult, but it reinforces the material better. Two word search puzzles have words only for students who find the clue puzzles too difficult.

CROSSWORD PUZZLES

Both unit and vocabulary word sections have 4 crossword puzzles.

BINGO CARDS

There are 32 individual bingo cards for the unit words and 32 individual bingo cards for the vocabulary words. You can use your word list as a "call list," calling the words at random and marking them off of your list as you go, or you could use the flash cards by cutting them apart and drawing the words at random from a hat (or box or whatever). To make a better review, you might ask for the definition and spelling of each word as you call it out–or you could call out the definitions and have students tell you the words they need to look for on the puzzle.

JUGGLE LETTERS

The vocabulary juggle letter game is intended to help students learn the spellings of the words. One sheet has the definitions listed on it as an extra help for students who need it or to reinforce the definitions if you choose to do so.

FLASH CARDS

We've included a set of vocabulary flash cards you can duplicate, cut, and fold for your students. Some teachers make a few sets for general use by the class; others make a set for each student. Some teachers duplicate them for each student and have the students cut & fold their own. You can cut out just the words and put them in a hat, have each student pick out one word and write the definition and a sentence for that word. Students then swap words and papers, with the next student adding a sentence of his own under the last one. You can have students swap as many times as you like. Each time the student will read the sentences written prior to his own and then add a sentence. You can cut out the words and definitions separately and play "I Have; Who Has?" Each student in the room draws a word and definition. The first student says, "I have (the name of the word). Who has the definition?" The student with the definition reads it then says, "I have (the name of the vocabulary word she has). Who has the definition?" The round continues until all words and definitions have been given.

Light in the Forest Word List

No.	Word	Clue/Definition
1.	ALEC	Cousin who gave his white man's clothes to True Son
2.	ALLEGHI	River where the boys stole the boat: ___ Sipu
3.	APPLE	True Son wanted to eat it to commit suicide: May ___
4.	ARROW	Cousin who accompanied True Son on his journeys: Half ___
5.	BANK	Thitpan's father-in-law who had only one eye: High-___
6.	BASKET	Bejance's occupation: ___ maker
7.	BEJANCE	Negro slave and basket maker
8.	BLACK	Half Arrow's father: ___ Fish
9.	BONE	A Shawano who went on the raid with Thitpan: Cheek ___
10.	BUTLER	Wanted to wear True Son's Indian clothes: Gordie ___
11.	CAPTAIN	Parson Elder's rank with the Paxton boys
12.	CHILDSLEY	Dr. who thought True Son's illness was due to miasmas and captivity
13.	CONESTOGO	Tribe of Indians massacred at Peshtank
14.	CORN	Indian rumored to live in the hills: ___ Blade
15.	CRANE	Was killed and scalped by Uncle Wilse: Little ___
16.	CUYLOGA	True Son's Indian father
17.	DELAWARE	Indian language True Son spoke
18.	DISBELIEVER	Blackened half of True Son's face
19.	ELEVEN	Number of years John Butler lived with the Indians
20.	FEBRUARY	The Month When the First Frog Croaks
21.	FEVER	True Son's illness caused by his captivity with whites
22.	FIFTEEN	True Son's age at the beginning of the story
23.	FLATBOAT	True Son warned its occupants of an ambush
24.	FOUR	Johnny's age when he was taken by the Indians
25.	GRAVE	True Son thought sleeping in a bed in a house was like this
26.	HARDY	Interpreter and guard: Del ___
27.	HARRY	True Son's white father
28.	HILL	Under-The-___ put white clay on half of True Son's face
29.	JANUARY	The Month When the Ground Squirrels Begin to Run
30.	JOHN	True Son's white name: ___ Cameron Butler
31.	KATE	Took True Son's Indian clothes away from him: Aunt ___
32.	LENNI	Tribe True Son belonged to: ___ Lenape
33.	MARCH	The Month of the Shad
34.	MASSACRE	What the Paxton boys did to the Conestogo Indians
35.	MECHELIT	True Son's older sister
36.	MUSKINGUM	River where the boys bathed when they returned to their tribe
37.	MYRA	True Son's white mother
38.	NOVEMBER	The Month of the First Snow
39.	OHIO	State in which the Tuscarawas River is located
40.	OWENS	Uncle George ___ tried to explain frontier justice to True Son
41.	PAINT	Tattooed warrior who went on the raid: Put-On-___
42.	PARSON	Peshtank captain; sacrificed Indian lives to save his favorite horse: ___ Elder
43.	PAXTON	Township where True Son was born and massacre took place
44.	PENNSYLVANIA	Location of Fort Pitt and Paxton Township
45.	PESHTANK	Indian name for Paxton
46.	PHILADELPHIA	City where Indians received sympathetic treatment
47.	PITT	Fort at western end of the white settlements
48.	PLAGUE	What True Son's life with the whites felt like to him
49.	QUAQUENGA	True Son's Indian mother
50.	RICHTER	Author
51.	SCALP	Thitpan had one that belonged to a white child
52.	SISTER	A'astonah was True Son's younger ___

Light in the Forest Word List Continued

No.	Word	Clue/Definition
53.	STOLEN	True Son and Half Arrrow's transportation down Ohio River: ___ boat
54.	SUSQUEHANNA	White people stole its land and graves from Cuyloga's tribe: ___ River
55.	THITPAN	Little Crane's brother who wanted to war against the whites
56.	TREE	Where True Son hid when he heard he was to return to the whites
57.	TRUE	Captured at 4 years of age & raised as an Indian: ___ Son
58.	TUSCARAWAS	River where Cuyloga's tribe lived
59.	WILSE	Uncle leader of Paxton boys; killed & scalped Little Crane
60.	YENGUE	Yankee; white settlers

Light in the Forest Fill In The Blank 1

_____ 1. True Son's white mother

_____ 2. Uncle George ___ tried to explain frontier justice to True Son

_____ 3. Peshtank captain; sacrificed Indian lives to save his favorite horse: ___ Elder

_____ 4. State in which the Tuscarawas River is located

_____ 5. Uncle leader of Paxton boys; killed & scalped Little Crane

_____ 6. Location of Fort Pitt and Paxton Township

_____ 7. True Son and Half Arrrow's transportation down Ohio River: ___ boat

_____ 8. True Son's illness caused by his captivity with whites

_____ 9. Township where True Son was born and massacre took place

_____ 10. Indian rumored to live in the hills: ___ Blade

_____ 11. Tribe True Son belonged to: ___ Lenape

_____ 12. True Son's white father

_____ 13. Tattooed warrior who went on the raid: Put-On-___

_____ 14. Interpreter and guard: Del ___

_____ 15. The Month When the First Frog Croaks

_____ 16. Indian language True Son spoke

_____ 17. A'astonah was True Son's younger ___

_____ 18. Author

_____ 19. Under-The-___ put white clay on half of True Son's face

_____ 20. City where Indians received sympathetic treatment

Light in the Forest Fill In The Blank 1 Answer Key

MYRA	1. True Son's white mother
OWENS	2. Uncle George ___ tried to explain frontier justice to True Son
PARSON	3. Peshtank captain; sacrificed Indian lives to save his favorite horse: ___ Elder
OHIO	4. State in which the Tuscarawas River is located
WILSE	5. Uncle leader of Paxton boys; killed & scalped Little Crane
PENNSYLVANIA	6. Location of Fort Pitt and Paxton Township
STOLEN	7. True Son and Half Arrrow's transportation down Ohio River: ___ boat
FEVER	8. True Son's illness caused by his captivity with whites
PAXTON	9. Township where True Son was born and massacre took place
CORN	10. Indian rumored to live in the hills: ___ Blade
LENNI	11. Tribe True Son belonged to: ___ Lenape
HARRY	12. True Son's white father
PAINT	13. Tattooed warrior who went on the raid: Put-On-___
HARDY	14. Interpreter and guard: Del ___
FEBRUARY	15. The Month When the First Frog Croaks
DELAWARE	16. Indian language True Son spoke
SISTER	17. A'astonah was True Son's younger ___
RICHTER	18. Author
HILL	19. Under-The-___ put white clay on half of True Son's face
PHILADELPHIA	20. City where Indians received sympathetic treatment

Light in the Forest Fill In The Blank 2

_____ 1. Captured at 4 years of ave & raised as an Indian: ___ Son

_____ 2. True Son's age at the beginning of the story

_____ 3. A Shawano who went on the raid with Thitpan: Cheek ___

_____ 4. Tattooed warrior who went on the raid: Put-On-___

_____ 5. Wanted to wear True Son's Indian clothes: Gordie ___

_____ 6. Number of years John Butler lived with the Indians

_____ 7. Cousin who gave his white man's clothes to True Son

_____ 8. True Son and Half Arrrow's transportation down Ohio River: ___ boat

_____ 9. Uncle George ___ tried to explain frontier justice to True Son

_____ 10. Thitpan had one that belonged to a white child

_____ 11. Township where True Son was born and massacre took place

_____ 12. Where True Son hid when he heard he was to return to the whites

_____ 13. River where the boys bathed when they returned to their tribe

_____ 14. Peshtank captain; sacrificed Indian lives to save his favorite horse: ___ Elder

_____ 15. City where Indians received sympathetic treatment

_____ 16. True Son warned its occupants of an ambush

_____ 17. What True Son's life with the whites felt like to him

_____ 18. The Month When the Ground Squirrels Begin to Run

_____ 19. Indian rumored to live in the hills: ___ Blade

_____ 20. Johnny's age when he was taken by the Indians

Light in the Forest Fill In The Blank 2 Answer Key

TRUE	1. Captured at 4 years of ave & raised as an Indian: ___ Son
FIFTEEN	2. True Son's age at the beginning of the story
BONE	3. A Shawano who went on the raid with Thitpan: Cheek ___
PAINT	4. Tattooed warrior who went on the raid: Put-On-___
BUTLER	5. Wanted to wear True Son's Indian clothes: Gordie ___
ELEVEN	6. Number of years John Butler lived with the Indians
ALEC	7. Cousin who gave his white man's clothes to True Son
STOLEN	8. True Son and Half Arrrow's transportation down Ohio River: ___ boat
OWENS	9. Uncle George ___ tried to explain frontier justice to True Son
SCALP	10. Thitpan had one that belonged to a white child
PAXTON	11. Township where True Son was born and massacre took place
TREE	12. Where True Son hid when he heard he was to return to the whites
MUSKINGUM	13. River where the boys bathed when they returned to their tribe
PARSON	14. Peshtank captain; sacrificed Indian lives to save his favorite horse: ___ Elder
PHILADELPHIA	15. City where Indians received sympathetic treatment
FLATBOAT	16. True Son warned its occupants of an ambush
PLAGUE	17. What True Son's life with the whites felt like to him
JANUARY	18. The Month When the Ground Squirrels Begin to Run
CORN	19. Indian rumored to live in the hills: ___ Blade
FOUR	20. Johnny's age when he was taken by the Indians

Light in the Forest Fill In The Blank 3

_____ 1. Tribe of Indians massacred at Peshtank

_____ 2. True Son thought sleeping in a bed in a house was like this

_____ 3. Took True Son's Indian clothes away from him: Aunt ___

_____ 4. Interpreter and guard: Del ___

_____ 5. Tattooed warrior who went on the raid: Put-On-___

_____ 6. Where True Son hid when he heard he was to return to the whites

_____ 7. True Son's Indian mother

_____ 8. Indian language True Son spoke

_____ 9. The Month of the Shad

_____ 10. What True Son's life with the whites felt like to him

_____ 11. River where the boys stole the boat: ___ Sipu

_____ 12. True Son's white name: ___ Cameron Butler

_____ 13. True Son's age at the beginning of the story

_____ 14. True Son's Indian father

_____ 15. Bejance's occupation: ___ maker

_____ 16. Township where True Son was born and massacre took place

_____ 17. City where Indians received sympathetic treatment

_____ 18. True Son's illness caused by his captivity with whites

_____ 19. Thitpan's father-in-law who had only one eye: High-___

_____ 20. Location of Fort Pitt and Paxton Township

Light in the Forest Fill In The Blank 3 Answer Key

CONESTOGO	1. Tribe of Indians massacred at Peshtank
GRAVE	2. True Son thought sleeping in a bed in a house was like this
KATE	3. Took True Son's Indian clothes away from him: Aunt ___
HARDY	4. Interpreter and guard: Del ___
PAINT	5. Tattooed warrior who went on the raid: Put-On-___
TREE	6. Where True Son hid when he heard he was to return to the whites
QUAQUENGA	7. True Son's Indian mother
DELAWARE	8. Indian language True Son spoke
MARCH	9. The Month of the Shad
PLAGUE	10. What True Son's life with the whites felt like to him
ALLEGHI	11. River where the boys stole the boat: ___ Sipu
JOHN	12. True Son's white name: ___ Cameron Butler
FIFTEEN	13. True Son's age at the beginning of the story
CUYLOGA	14. True Son's Indian father
BASKET	15. Bejance's occupation: ___ maker
PAXTON	16. Township where True Son was born and massacre took place
PHILADELPHIA	17. City where Indians received sympathetic treatment
FEVER	18. True Son's illness caused by his captivity with whites
BANK	19. Thitpan's father-in-law who had only one eye: High-___
PENNSYLVANIA	20. Location of Fort Pitt and Paxton Township

Light in the Forest Fill In The Blank 4

_____ 1. A Shawano who went on the raid with Thitpan: Cheek ___

_____ 2. The Month When the Ground Squirrels Begin to Run

_____ 3. Yankee; white settlers

_____ 4. Half Arrow's father: ___ Fish

_____ 5. True Son warned its occupants of an ambush

_____ 6. Township where True Son was born and massacre took place

_____ 7. Took True Son's Indian clothes away from him: Aunt ___

_____ 8. True Son's Indian father

_____ 9. Parson Elder's rank with the Paxton boys

_____ 10. Bejance's occupation: ___ maker

_____ 11. Location of Fort Pitt and Paxton Township

_____ 12. Little Crane's brother who wanted to war against the whites

_____ 13. Indian language True Son spoke

_____ 14. Thitpan had one that belonged to a white child

_____ 15. Uncle George ___ tried to explain frontier justice to True Son

_____ 16. Wanted to wear True Son's Indian clothes: Gordie ___

_____ 17. Fort at western end of the white settlements

_____ 18. Under-The-___ put white clay on half of True Son's face

_____ 19. River where Cuyloga's tribe lived

_____ 20. Was killed and scalped by Uncle Wilse: Little ___

Light in the Forest Fill In The Blank 4 Answer Key

Word	#	Clue
BONE	1.	A Shawano who went on the raid with Thitpan: Cheek ___
JANUARY	2.	The Month When the Ground Squirrels Begin to Run
YENGUE	3.	Yankee; white settlers
BLACK	4.	Half Arrow's father: ___ Fish
FLATBOAT	5.	True Son warned its occupants of an ambush
PAXTON	6.	Township where True Son was born and massacre took place
KATE	7.	Took True Son's Indian clothes away from him: Aunt ___
CUYLOGA	8.	True Son's Indian father
CAPTAIN	9.	Parson Elder's rank with the Paxton boys
BASKET	10.	Bejance's occupation: ___ maker
PENNSYLVANIA	11.	Location of Fort Pitt and Paxton Township
THITPAN	12.	Little Crane's brother who wanted to war against the whites
DELAWARE	13.	Indian language True Son spoke
SCALP	14.	Thitpan had one that belonged to a white child
OWENS	15.	Uncle George ___ tried to explain frontier justice to True Son
BUTLER	16.	Wanted to wear True Son's Indian clothes: Gordie ___
PITT	17.	Fort at western end of the white settlements
HILL	18.	Under-The-___ put white clay on half of True Son's face
TUSCARAWAS	19.	River where Cuyloga's tribe lived
CRANE	20.	Was killed and scalped by Uncle Wilse: Little ___

Light in the Forest Matching 1

___ 1. BUTLER   A. Negro slave and basket maker
___ 2. HARDY   B. Wanted to wear True Son's Indian clothes: Gordie ___
___ 3. GRAVE   C. Uncle George ___ tried to explain frontier justice to True Son
___ 4. MYRA   D. Yankee; white settlers
___ 5. MASSACRE   E. True Son's age at the beginning of the story
___ 6. THITPAN   F. What the Paxton boys did to the Conestogo Indians
___ 7. CONESTOGO   G. Half Arrow's father: ___ Fish
___ 8. BANK   H. Peshtank captain; sacrificed Indian lives to save his favorite horse: ___ Elder
___ 9. FOUR   I. True Son's illness caused by his captivity with whites
___ 10. ELEVEN   J. River where Cuyloga's tribe lived
___ 11. YENGUE   K. A'astonah was True Son's younger ___
___ 12. BEJANCE   L. Thitpan had one that belonged to a white child
___ 13. MUSKINGUM   M. Thitpan's father-in-law who had only one eye: High-___
___ 14. SCALP   N. Interpreter and guard: Del ___
___ 15. LENNI   O. Tribe True Son belonged to: ___ Lenape
___ 16. DISBELIEVER   P. True Son thought sleeping in a bed in a house was like this
___ 17. ARROW   Q. True Son's white mother
___ 18. FEVER   R. Cousin who accompanied True Son on his journeys: Half ___
___ 19. BLACK   S. Number of years John Butler lived with the Indians
___ 20. SISTER   T. Johnny's age when he was taken by the Indians
___ 21. FIFTEEN   U. Tribe of Indians massacred at Peshtank
___ 22. CAPTAIN   V. Blackened half of True Son's face
___ 23. OWENS   W. Little Crane's brother who wanted to war against the whites
___ 24. TUSCARAWAS   X. Parson Elder's rank with the Paxton boys
___ 25. PARSON   Y. River where the boys bathed when they returned to their tribe

Light in the Forest Matching 1 Answer Key

B - 1. BUTLER	A.	Negro slave and basket maker
N - 2. HARDY	B.	Wanted to wear True Son's Indian clothes: Gordie ___
P - 3. GRAVE	C.	Uncle George ___ tried to explain frontier justice to True Son
Q - 4. MYRA	D.	Yankee; white settlers
F - 5. MASSACRE	E.	True Son's age at the beginning of the story
W - 6. THITPAN	F.	What the Paxton boys did to the Conestogo Indians
U - 7. CONESTOGO	G.	Half Arrow's father: ___ Fish
M - 8. BANK	H.	Peshtank captain; sacrificed Indian lives to save his favorite horse: ___ Elder
T - 9. FOUR	I.	True Son's illness caused by his captivity with whites
S - 10. ELEVEN	J.	River where Cuyloga's tribe lived
D - 11. YENGUE	K.	A'astonah was True Son's younger ___
A - 12. BEJANCE	L.	Thitpan had one that belonged to a white child
Y - 13. MUSKINGUM	M.	Thitpan's father-in-law who had only one eye: High-___
L - 14. SCALP	N.	Interpreter and guard: Del ___
O - 15. LENNI	O.	Tribe True Son belonged to: ___ Lenape
V - 16. DISBELIEVER	P.	True Son thought sleeping in a bed in a house was like this
R - 17. ARROW	Q.	True Son's white mother
I - 18. FEVER	R.	Cousin who accompanied True Son on his journeys: Half ___
G - 19. BLACK	S.	Number of years John Butler lived with the Indians
K - 20. SISTER	T.	Johnny's age when he was taken by the Indians
E - 21. FIFTEEN	U.	Tribe of Indians massacred at Peshtank
X - 22. CAPTAIN	V.	Blackened half of True Son's face
C - 23. OWENS	W.	Little Crane's brother who wanted to war against the whites
J - 24. TUSCARAWAS	X.	Parson Elder's rank with the Paxton boys
H - 25. PARSON	Y.	River where the boys bathed when they returned to their tribe

15
Copyrighted

Light in the Forest Matching 2

___ 1. BASKET
___ 2. CRANE
___ 3. FLATBOAT
___ 4. PENNSYLVANIA
___ 5. FEVER
___ 6. WILSE
___ 7. HILL
___ 8. CHILDSLEY
___ 9. FEBRUARY
___ 10. OHIO
___ 11. BANK
___ 12. OWENS
___ 13. JOHN
___ 14. DELAWARE
___ 15. MECHELIT
___ 16. CORN
___ 17. FOUR
___ 18. THITPAN
___ 19. ELEVEN
___ 20. PHILADELPHIA
___ 21. CAPTAIN
___ 22. BUTLER
___ 23. TREE
___ 24. SISTER
___ 25. MARCH

A. Was killed and scalped by Uncle Wilse: Little ___
B. The Month of the Shad
C. City where Indians received sympathetic treatment
D. Uncle leader of Paxton boys; killed & scalped Little Crane
E. Dr. who thought True Son's illness was due to miasmas and captivity
F. Indian language True Son spoke
G. True Son warned its occupants of an ambush
H. True Son's white name: ___ Cameron Butler
I. True Son's older sister
J. Bejance's occupation: ___ maker
K. Parson Elder's rank with the Paxton boys
L. Where True Son hid when he heard he was to return to the whites
M. State in which the Tuscarawas River is located
N. Johnny's age when he was taken by the Indians
O. Under-The-___ put white clay on half of True Son's face
P. The Month When the First Frog Croaks
Q. A'astonah was True Son's younger ___
R. True Son's illness caused by his captivity with whites
S. Thitpan's father-in-law who had only one eye: High-___
T. Uncle George ___ tried to explain frontier justice to True Son
U. Little Crane's brother who wanted to war against the whites
V. Indian rumored to live in the hills: ___ Blade
W. Location of Fort Pitt and Paxton Township
X. Number of years John Butler lived with the Indians
Y. Wanted to wear True Son's Indian clothes: Gordie ___

Light in the Forest Matching 2 Answer Key

J - 1.	BASKET	A.	Was killed and scalped by Uncle Wilse: Little ___
A - 2.	CRANE	B.	The Month of the Shad
G - 3.	FLATBOAT	C.	City where Indians received sympathetic treatment
W - 4.	PENNSYLVANIA	D.	Uncle leader of Paxton boys; killed & scalped Little Crane
R - 5.	FEVER	E.	Dr. who thought True Son's illness was due to miasmas and captivity
D - 6.	WILSE	F.	Indian language True Son spoke
O - 7.	HILL	G.	True Son warned its occupants of an ambush
E - 8.	CHILDSLEY	H.	True Son's white name: ___ Cameron Butler
P - 9.	FEBRUARY	I.	True Son's older sister
M -10.	OHIO	J.	Bejance's occupation: ___ maker
S -11.	BANK	K.	Parson Elder's rank with the Paxton boys
T -12.	OWENS	L.	Where True Son hid when he heard he was to return to the whites
H -13.	JOHN	M.	State in which the Tuscarawas River is located
F -14.	DELAWARE	N.	Johnny's age when he was taken by the Indians
I -15.	MECHELIT	O.	Under-The-___ put white clay on half of True Son's face
V -16.	CORN	P.	The Month When the First Frog Croaks
N -17.	FOUR	Q.	A'astonah was True Son's younger ___
U -18.	THITPAN	R.	True Son's illness caused by his captivity with whites
X -19.	ELEVEN	S.	Thitpan's father-in-law who had only one eye: High-___
C -20.	PHILADELPHIA	T.	Uncle George ___ tried to explain frontier justice to True Son
K -21.	CAPTAIN	U.	Little Crane's brother who wanted to war against the whites
Y -22.	BUTLER	V.	Indian rumored to live in the hills: ___ Blade
L -23.	TREE	W.	Location of Fort Pitt and Paxton Township
Q -24.	SISTER	X.	Number of years John Butler lived with the Indians
B -25.	MARCH	Y.	Wanted to wear True Son's Indian clothes: Gordie ___

Light in the Forest Matching 3

___ 1. OWENS
___ 2. PARSON
___ 3. FLATBOAT
___ 4. ALLEGHI
___ 5. SISTER
___ 6. HARDY
___ 7. ARROW
___ 8. MUSKINGUM
___ 9. BEJANCE
___ 10. DISBELIEVER
___ 11. LENNI
___ 12. TUSCARAWAS
___ 13. MASSACRE
___ 14. KATE
___ 15. MARCH
___ 16. QUAQUENGA
___ 17. DELAWARE
___ 18. BASKET
___ 19. SUSQUEHANNA
___ 20. ELEVEN
___ 21. JANUARY
___ 22. FEBRUARY
___ 23. HILL
___ 24. JOHN
___ 25. CONESTOGO

A. Negro slave and basket maker
B. A'astonah was True Son's younger ___
C. River where the boys stole the boat: ___ Sipu
D. White people stole its land and graves from Cuyloga's tribe: ___ River
E. Indian language True Son spoke
F. True Son warned its occupants of an ambush
G. Under-The-___ put white clay on half of True Son's face
H. The Month of the Shad
I. Bejance's occupation: ___ maker
J. River where the boys bathed when they returned to their tribe
K. Blackened half of True Son's face
L. True Son's Indian mother
M. The Month When the Ground Squirrels Begin to Run
N. Number of years John Butler lived with the Indians
O. Peshtank captain; sacrificed Indian lives to save his favorite horse: ___ Elder
P. The Month When the First Frog Croaks
Q. Took True Son's Indian clothes away from him: Aunt ___
R. Cousin who accompanied True Son on his journeys: Half ___
S. Tribe of Indians massacred at Peshtank
T. What the Paxton boys did to the Conestogo Indians
U. River where Cuyloga's tribe lived
V. True Son's white name: ___ Cameron Butler
W. Uncle George ___ tried to explain frontier justice to True Son
X. Tribe True Son belonged to: ___ Lenape
Y. Interpreter and guard: Del ___

Light in the Forest Matching 3 Answer Key

W - 1.	OWENS	A. Negro slave and basket maker
O - 2.	PARSON	B. A'astonah was True Son's younger ___
F - 3.	FLATBOAT	C. River where the boys stole the boat: ___ Sipu
C - 4.	ALLEGHI	D. White people stole its land and graves from Cuyloga's tribe: ___ River
B - 5.	SISTER	E. Indian language True Son spoke
Y - 6.	HARDY	F. True Son warned its occupants of an ambush
R - 7.	ARROW	G. Under-The-___ put white clay on half of True Son's face
J - 8.	MUSKINGUM	H. The Month of the Shad
A - 9.	BEJANCE	I. Bejance's occupation: ___ maker
K - 10.	DISBELIEVER	J. River where the boys bathed when they returned to their tribe
X - 11.	LENNI	K. Blackened half of True Son's face
U - 12.	TUSCARAWAS	L. True Son's Indian mother
T - 13.	MASSACRE	M. The Month When the Ground Squirrels Begin to Run
Q - 14.	KATE	N. Number of years John Butler lived with the Indians
H - 15.	MARCH	O. Peshtank captain; sacrificed Indian lives to save his favorite horse: ___ Elder
L - 16.	QUAQUENGA	P. The Month When the First Frog Croaks
E - 17.	DELAWARE	Q. Took True Son's Indian clothes away from him: Aunt ___
I - 18.	BASKET	R. Cousin who accompanied True Son on his journeys: Half ___
D - 19.	SUSQUEHANNA	S. Tribe of Indians massacred at Peshtank
N - 20.	ELEVEN	T. What the Paxton boys did to the Conestogo Indians
M - 21.	JANUARY	U. River where Cuyloga's tribe lived
P - 22.	FEBRUARY	V. True Son's white name: ___ Cameron Butler
G - 23.	HILL	W. Uncle George ___ tried to explain frontier justice to True Son
V - 24.	JOHN	X. Tribe True Son belonged to: ___ Lenape
S - 25.	CONESTOGO	Y. Interpreter and guard: Del ___

Light in the Forest Matching 4

___ 1. THITPAN   A. Tattooed warrior who went on the raid: Put-On-___
___ 2. HILL   B. Indian language True Son spoke
___ 3. CUYLOGA   C. Negro slave and basket maker
___ 4. PAINT   D. True Son's white father
___ 5. GRAVE   E. City where Indians received sympathetic treatment
___ 6. PHILADELPHIA   F. The Month of the Shad
___ 7. ALEC   G. Uncle George ___ tried to explain frontier justice to True Son
___ 8. BUTLER   H. Wanted to wear True Son's Indian clothes: Gordie ___
___ 9. BANK   I. State in which the Tuscarawas River is located
___ 10. MARCH   J. True Son thought sleeping in a bed in a house was like this
___ 11. SISTER   K. Tribe of Indians massacred at Peshtank
___ 12. CRANE   L. A'astonah was True Son's younger ___
___ 13. BEJANCE   M. The Month When the First Frog Croaks
___ 14. OHIO   N. Was killed and scalped by Uncle Wilse: Little ___
___ 15. FEBRUARY   O. Blackened half of True Son's face
___ 16. DISBELIEVER   P. River where Cuyloga's tribe lived
___ 17. OWENS   Q. Location of Fort Pitt and Paxton Township
___ 18. PENNSYLVANIA   R. White people stole its land and graves from Cuyloga's tribe: ___ River
___ 19. PESHTANK   S. Took True Son's Indian clothes away from him: Aunt ___
___ 20. HARRY   T. Little Crane's brother who wanted to war against the whites
___ 21. SUSQUEHANNA   U. True Son's Indian father
___ 22. KATE   V. Indian name for Paxton
___ 23. DELAWARE   W. Cousin who gave his white man's clothes to True Son
___ 24. TUSCARAWAS   X. Thitpan's father-in-law who had only one eye: High-___
___ 25. CONESTOGO   Y. Under-The-___ put white clay on half of True Son's face

Light in the Forest Matching 4 Answer Key

T - 1. THITPAN	A.	Tattooed warrior who went on the raid: Put-On-___
Y - 2. HILL	B.	Indian language True Son spoke
U - 3. CUYLOGA	C.	Negro slave and basket maker
A - 4. PAINT	D.	True Son's white father
J - 5. GRAVE	E.	City where Indians received sympathetic treatment
E - 6. PHILADELPHIA	F.	The Month of the Shad
W - 7. ALEC	G.	Uncle George ___ tried to explain frontier justice to True Son
H - 8. BUTLER	H.	Wanted to wear True Son's Indian clothes: Gordie ___
X - 9. BANK	I.	State in which the Tuscarawas River is located
F - 10. MARCH	J.	True Son thought sleeping in a bed in a house was like this
L - 11. SISTER	K.	Tribe of Indians massacred at Peshtank
N - 12. CRANE	L.	A'astonah was True Son's younger ___
C - 13. BEJANCE	M.	The Month When the First Frog Croaks
I - 14. OHIO	N.	Was killed and scalped by Uncle Wilse: Little ___
M - 15. FEBRUARY	O.	Blackened half of True Son's face
O - 16. DISBELIEVER	P.	River where Cuyloga's tribe lived
G - 17. OWENS	Q.	Location of Fort Pitt and Paxton Township
Q - 18. PENNSYLVANIA	R.	White people stole its land and graves from Cuyloga's tribe: ___ River
V - 19. PESHTANK	S.	Took True Son's Indian clothes away from him: Aunt ___
D - 20. HARRY	T.	Little Crane's brother who wanted to war against the whites
R - 21. SUSQUEHANNA	U.	True Son's Indian father
S - 22. KATE	V.	Indian name for Paxton
B - 23. DELAWARE	W.	Cousin who gave his white man's clothes to True Son
P - 24. TUSCARAWAS	X.	Thitpan's father-in-law who had only one eye: High-___
K - 25. CONESTOGO	Y.	Under-The-___ put white clay on half of True Son's face

Light in the Forest Magic Squares 1

Match the definition with the vocabulary word. Put your answers in the magic squares below. When your answers are correct, all columns and rows will add to the same number.

A. PITT
B. PARSON
C. HARDY
D. BLACK
E. GRAVE
F. LENNI
G. MARCH
H. MUSKINGUM
I. PHILADELPHIA
J. QUAQUENGA
K. PAXTON
L. FOUR
M. CRANE
N. FLATBOAT
O. JOHN
P. DELAWARE

1. River where the boys bathed when they returned to their tribe
2. Was killed and scalped by Uncle Wilse: Little ___
3. Peshtank captain; sacrificed Indian lives to save his favorite horse: ___ Elder
4. Township where True Son was born and massacre took place
5. True Son's Indian mother
6. Interpreter and guard: Del ___
7. Indian language True Son spoke
8. True Son thought sleeping in a bed in a house was like this
9. True Son's white name: ___ Cameron Butler
10. Tribe True Son belonged to: ___ Lenape
11. City where Indians received sympathetic treatment
12. Half Arrow's father: ___ Fish
13. Fort at western end of the white settlements
14. Johnny's age when he was taken by the Indians
15. The Month of the Shad
16. True Son warned its occupants of an ambush

A=	B=	C=	D=
E=	F=	G=	H=
I=	J=	K=	L=
M=	N=	O=	P=

Light in the Forest Magic Squares 1 Answer Key

Match the definition with the vocabulary word. Put your answers in the magic squares below. When your answers are correct, all columns and rows will add to the same number.

A. PITT
B. PARSON
C. HARDY
D. BLACK
E. GRAVE
F. LENNI
G. MARCH
H. MUSKINGUM
I. PHILADELPHIA
J. QUAQUENGA
K. PAXTON
L. FOUR
M. CRANE
N. FLATBOAT
O. JOHN
P. DELAWARE

1. River where the boys bathed when they returned to their tribe
2. Was killed and scalped by Uncle Wilse: Little ___
3. Peshtank captain; sacrificed Indian lives to save his favorite horse: ___ Elder
4. Township where True Son was born and massacre took place
5. True Son's Indian mother
6. Interpreter and guard: Del ___
7. Indian language True Son spoke
8. True Son thought sleeping in a bed in a house was like this
9. True Son's white name: ___ Cameron Butler
10. Tribe True Son belonged to: ___ Lenape
11. City where Indians received sympathetic treatment
12. Half Arrow's father: ___ Fish
13. Fort at western end of the white settlements
14. Johnny's age when he was taken by the Indians
15. The Month of the Shad
16. True Son warned its occupants of an ambush

A=13	B=3	C=6	D=12
E=8	F=10	G=15	H=1
I=11	J=5	K=4	L=14
M=2	N=16	O=9	P=7

Light in the Forest Magic Squares 2

Match the definition with the vocabulary word. Put your answers in the magic squares below. When your answers are correct, all columns and rows will add to the same number.

A. CRANE
B. RICHTER
C. PENNSYLVANIA
D. YENGUE
E. CUYLOGA
F. QUAQUENGA
G. PITT
H. FIFTEEN
I. PAXTON
J. GRAVE
K. PLAGUE
L. FEVER
M. CHILDSLEY
N. PARSON
O. NOVEMBER
P. OWENS

1. The Month of the First Snow
2. True Son thought sleeping in a bed in a house was like this
3. True Son's age at the beginning of the story
4. Was killed and scalped by Uncle Wilse: Little ___
5. Yankee; white settlers
6. True Son's Indian father
7. What True Son's life with the whites felt like to him
8. Peshtank captain; sacrificed Indian lives to save his favorite horse: ___ Elder
9. True Son's Indian mother
10. Location of Fort Pitt and Paxton Township
11. Dr. who thought True Son's illness was due to miasmas and captivity
12. True Son's illness caused by his captivity with whites
13. Township where True Son was born and massacre took place
14. Uncle George ___ tried to explain frontier justice to True Son
15. Author
16. Fort at western end of the white settlements

A=	B=	C=	D=
E=	F=	G=	H=
I=	J=	K=	L=
M=	N=	O=	P=

Light in the Forest Magic Squares 2 Answer Key

Match the definition with the vocabulary word. Put your answers in the magic squares below. When your answers are correct, all columns and rows will add to the same number.

A. CRANE
B. RICHTER
C. PENNSYLVANIA
D. YENGUE
E. CUYLOGA
F. QUAQUENGA
G. PITT
H. FIFTEEN
I. PAXTON
J. GRAVE
K. PLAGUE
L. FEVER
M. CHILDSLEY
N. PARSON
O. NOVEMBER
P. OWENS

1. The Month of the First Snow
2. True Son thought sleeping in a bed in a house was like this
3. True Son's age at the beginning of the story
4. Was killed and scalped by Uncle Wilse: Little ___
5. Yankee; white settlers
6. True Son's Indian father
7. What True Son's life with the whites felt like to him
8. Peshtank captain; sacrificed Indian lives to save his favorite horse: ___ Elder
9. True Son's Indian mother
10. Location of Fort Pitt and Paxton Township
11. Dr. who thought True Son's illness was due to miasmas and captivity
12. True Son's illness caused by his captivity with whites
13. Township where True Son was born and massacre took place
14. Uncle George ___ tried to explain frontier justice to True Son
15. Author
16. Fort at western end of the white settlements

A=4	B=15	C=10	D=5
E=6	F=9	G=16	H=3
I=13	J=2	K=7	L=12
M=11	N=8	O=1	P=14

Light in the Forest Magic Squares 3

Match the definition with the vocabulary word. Put your answers in the magic squares below. When your answers are correct, all columns and rows will add to the same number.

A. TREE   E. MECHELIT   I. MUSKINGUM   M. FOUR
B. BEJANCE   F. BASKET   J. JANUARY   N. CUYLOGA
C. ALEC   G. JOHN   K. ELEVEN   O. TRUE
D. FEVER   H. SUSQUEHANNA   L. FIFTEEN   P. RICHTER

1. White people stole its land and graves from Cuyloga's tribe: ___ River
2. Where True Son hid when he heard he was to return to the whites
3. Negro slave and basket maker
4. True Son's white name: ___ Cameron Butler
5. The Month When the Ground Squirrels Begin to Run
6. Captured at 4 years of age & raised as an Indian: ___ Son
7. Author
8. River where the boys bathed when they returned to their tribe
9. Number of years John Butler lived with the Indians
10. True Son's Indian father
11. Johnny's age when he was taken by the Indians
12. True Son's age at the beginning of the story
13. True Son's older sister
14. True Son's illness caused by his captivity with whites
15. Cousin who gave his white man's clothes to True Son
16. Bejance's occupation: ___ maker

A= 2	B= 3	C= 15	D= 14
E= 13	F= 16	G= 4	H= 1
I= 8	J= 5	K= 9	L= 12
M= 11	N= 10	O= 6	P= 7

Light in the Forest Magic Squares 3 Answer Key

Match the definition with the vocabulary word. Put your answers in the magic squares below. When your answers are correct, all columns and rows will add to the same number.

A. TREE
B. BEJANCE
C. ALEC
D. FEVER
E. MECHELIT
F. BASKET
G. JOHN
H. SUSQUEHANNA
I. MUSKINGUM
J. JANUARY
K. ELEVEN
L. FIFTEEN
M. FOUR
N. CUYLOGA
O. TRUE
P. RICHTER

1. White people stole its land and graves from Cuyloga's tribe: ___ River
2. Where True Son hid when he heard he was to return to the whites
3. Negro slave and basket maker
4. True Son's white name: ___ Cameron Butler
5. The Month When the Ground Squirrels Begin to Run
6. Captured at 4 years of age & raised as an Indian: ___ Son
7. Author
8. River where the boys bathed when they returned to their tribe
9. Number of years John Butler lived with the Indians
10. True Son's Indian father
11. Johnny's age when he was taken by the Indians
12. True Son's age at the beginning of the story
13. True Son's older sister
14. True Son's illness caused by his captivity with whites
15. Cousin who gave his white man's clothes to True Son
16. Bejance's occupation: ___ maker

A=2	B=3	C=15	D=14
E=13	F=16	G=4	H=1
I=8	J=5	K=9	L=12
M=11	N=10	O=6	P=7

Light in the Forest Magic Squares 4

Match the definition with the vocabulary word. Put your answers in the magic squares below. When your answers are correct, all columns and rows will add to the same number.

A. MUSKINGUM   E. FLATBOAT   I. BLACK   M. FEBRUARY
B. OWENS   F. CONESTOGO   J. PESHTANK   N. TREE
C. FOUR   G. ARROW   K. OHIO   O. CAPTAIN
D. SCALP   H. ALLEGHI   L. MASSACRE   P. APPLE

1. Uncle George ___ tried to explain frontier justice to True Son
2. Cousin who accompanied True Son on his journeys: Half ___
3. State in which the Tuscarawas River is located
4. Where True Son hid when he heard he was to return to the whites
5. The Month When the First Frog Croaks
6. What the Paxton boys did to the Conestogo Indians
7. River where the boys stole the boat: ___ Sipu
8. River where the boys bathed when they returned to their tribe
9. True Son wanted to eat it to commit suicide: May ___
10. Half Arrow's father: ___ Fish
11. True Son warned its occupants of an ambush
12. Thitpan had one that belonged to a white child
13. Johnny's age when he was taken by the Indians
14. Tribe of Indians massacred at Peshtank
15. Indian name for Paxton
16. Parson Elder's rank with the Paxton boys

A=	B=	C=	D=
E=	F=	G=	H=
I=	J=	K=	L=
M=	N=	O=	P=

28
Copyrighted

Light in the Forest Magic Squares 4 Answer Key

Match the definition with the vocabulary word. Put your answers in the magic squares below. When your answers are correct, all columns and rows will add to the same number.

A. MUSKINGUM E. FLATBOAT   I. BLACK   M. FEBRUARY
B. OWENS   F. CONESTOGO J. PESHTANK   N. TREE
C. FOUR   G. ARROW   K. OHIO   O. CAPTAIN
D. SCALP   H. ALLEGHI   L. MASSACRE   P. APPLE

1. Uncle George ___ tried to explain frontier justice to True Son
2. Cousin who accompanied True Son on his journeys: Half ___
3. State in which the Tuscarawas River is located
4. Where True Son hid when he heard he was to return to the whites
5. The Month When the First Frog Croaks
6. What the Paxton boys did to the Conestogo Indians
7. River where the boys stole the boat: ___ Sipu
8. River where the boys bathed when they returned to their tribe
9. True Son wanted to eat it to commit suicide: May ___
10. Half Arrow's father: ___ Fish
11. True Son warned its occupants of an ambush
12. Thitpan had one that belonged to a white child
13. Johnny's age when he was taken by the Indians
14. Tribe of Indians massacred at Peshtank
15. Indian name for Paxton
16. Parson Elder's rank with the Paxton boys

A=8	B=1	C=13	D=12
E=11	F=14	G=2	H=7
I=10	J=15	K=3	L=6
M=5	N=4	O=16	P=9

Light in the Forest Word Search 1

```
K P G C Q S P E S H T A N K Z D
N D L Y H D T C B C D X L W P Y
H X M A T I J C A X F J N Y T W
L D N V G Z L G V P S W D N R G
P G G B C U J D B G T G H L N G
M X Z H S R E E S N S A X E A N
X J T F E R H L B L B F I N P G
M Z W L E F T A E L E V E N T S
V N T T M N Y W Y Y N Y O I I F
W U S Z A D E A R Y K T V X H V
B I E E R T T R C A X S E C T W
S Z L A C N A E R A N U E T O R
K B H S H H K Y P E G L I R D J
Q C S P E O M X W N A P R W J F
G R A V E J G O E C N A J E B S
P A R S O N H Y F L A T B O A T
```

A'astonah was True Son's younger ___ (6)
Cousin who accompanied True Son on his journeys: Half ___ (5)
Cousin who gave his white man's clothes to True Son (4)
Dr. who thought True Son's illness was due to miasmas and captivity (9)
Fort at western end of the white settlements (4)
Indian language True Son spoke (8)
Indian name for Paxton (8)
Interpreter and guard: Del ___ (5)
Little Crane's brother who wanted to war against the whites (7)
Negro slave and basket maker (7)
Number of years John Butler lived with the Indians (6)
Parson Elder's rank with the Paxton boys (7)
Peshtank captain; sacrificed Indian lives to save his favorite horse: ___ Elder (6)
The Month of the Shad (5)
Took True Son's Indian clothes away from him: Aunt ___ (4)
Township where True Son was born and massacre took place (6)
Tribe True Son belonged to: ___ Lenape (5)

True Son thought sleeping in a bed in a house was like this (5)
True Son warned its occupants of an ambush (8)
True Son's white father (5)
True Son's white mother (4)
True Son's white name: ___ Cameron Butler (4)
Uncle George ___ tried to explain frontier justice to True Son (5)
Uncle leader of Paxton boys; killed & scalped Little Crane (5)
Wanted to wear True Son's Indian clothes: Gordie ___ (6)
What True Son's life with the whites felt like to him (6)
Where True Son hid when he heard he was to return to the whites (4)
Yankee; white settlers (6)

Light in the Forest Word Search 1 Answer Key

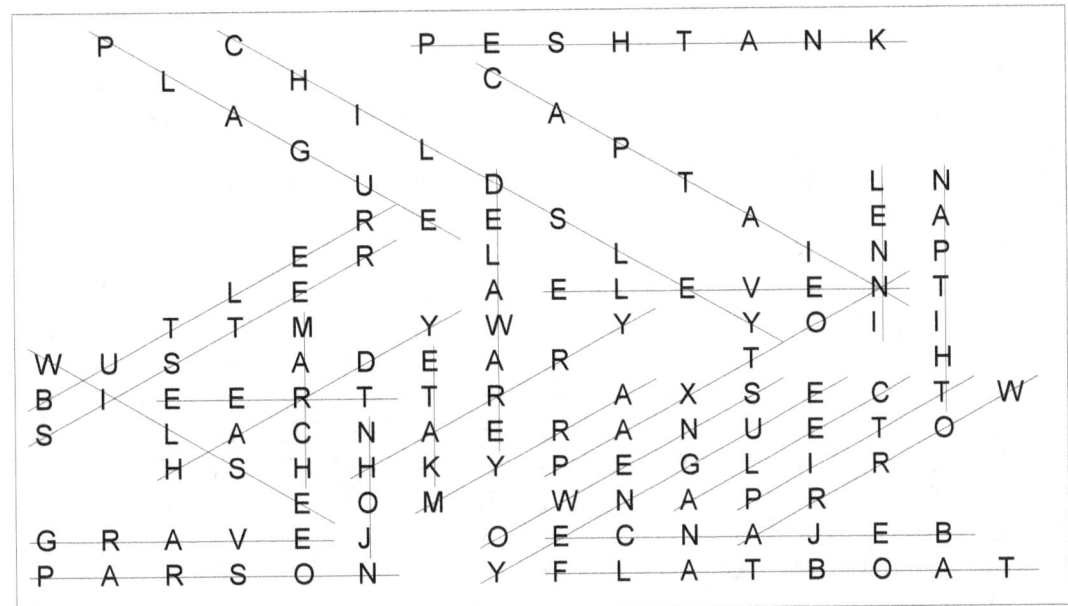

A'astonah was True Son's younger ___ (6)
Cousin who accompanied True Son on his journeys: Half ___ (5)
Cousin who gave his white man's clothes to True Son (4)
Dr. who thought True Son's illness was due to miasmas and captivity (9)
Fort at western end of the white settlements (4)
Indian language True Son spoke (8)
Indian name for Paxton (8)
Interpreter and guard: Del ___ (5)
Little Crane's brother who wanted to war against the whites (7)
Negro slave and basket maker (7)
Number of years John Butler lived with the Indians (6)
Parson Elder's rank with the Paxton boys (7)
Peshtank captain; sacrificed Indian lives to save his favorite horse: ___ Elder (6)
The Month of the Shad (5)
Took True Son's Indian clothes away from him: Aunt ___ (4)
Township where True Son was born and massacre took place (6)
Tribe True Son belonged to: ___ Lenape (5)

True Son thought sleeping in a bed in a house was like this (5)
True Son warned its occupants of an ambush (8)
True Son's white father (5)
True Son's white mother (4)
True Son's white name: ___ Cameron Butler (4)
Uncle George ___ tried to explain frontier justice to True Son (5)
Uncle leader of Paxton boys; killed & scalped Little Crane (5)
Wanted to wear True Son's Indian clothes: Gordie ___ (6)
What True Son's life with the whites felt like to him (6)
Where True Son hid when he heard he was to return to the whites (4)
Yankee; white settlers (6)

Light in the Forest Word Search 2

```
J D K L F C H I L D S L E Y Q T
A Q S P K P H B F I F T E E N H
N S A G N E U Q A U Q K W B D I
U V P R Q Q M C W S N A R R K T
A Y M H K X Y F H B K T X K J P
R S L J D R E K Y S Z E M Y R A
Y W H M A B Y D T W L X T T X N
H P C B R L P O E L A W A R E
B P R U J Q L E V T D O F K T W
S C A L P E H E S L I W O R R A
S R M I N A N T G H P G U S X Y
Y Y C O N A X Y O H T E R N Q G
R W B Z R T D T G P I A F W G W
K Y G C V R S L O B I V N W K L
B Q V J A R F V H N R T K K D D
S G Z H M E C H E L I T T P J F
```

A Shawano who went on the raid with Thitpan: Cheek ___ (4)
Bejance's occupation: ___ maker (6)
Captured at 4 years of age & raised as an Indian: ___ Son (4)
Cousin who accompanied True Son on his journeys: Half ___ (5)
Dr. who thought True Son's illness was due to miasmas and captivity (9)
Fort at western end of the white settlements (4)
Indian language True Son spoke (8)
Indian name for Paxton (8)
Interpreter and guard: Del ___ (5)
Johnny's age when he was taken by the Indians (4)
Little Crane's brother who wanted to war against the whites (7)
Number of years John Butler lived with the Indians (6)
River where the boys stole the boat: ___ Sipu (7)
State in which the Tuscarawas River is located (4)
Tattooed warrior who went on the raid: Put-On-___ (5)
The Month When the First Frog Croaks (8)
The Month When the Ground Squirrels Begin to Run (7)
The Month of the Shad (5)
Thitpan had one that belonged to a white child (5)
Took True Son's Indian clothes away from him: Aunt ___ (4)
Township where True Son was born and massacre took place (6)
True Son and Half Arrrow's transportation down Ohio River: ___ boat (6)
True Son's Indian mother (9)
True Son's age at the beginning of the story (7)
True Son's older sister (8)
True Son's white mother (4)
Uncle leader of Paxton boys; killed & scalped Little Crane (5)
Was killed and scalped by Uncle Wilse: Little ___ (5)

Light in the Forest Word Search 2 Answer Key

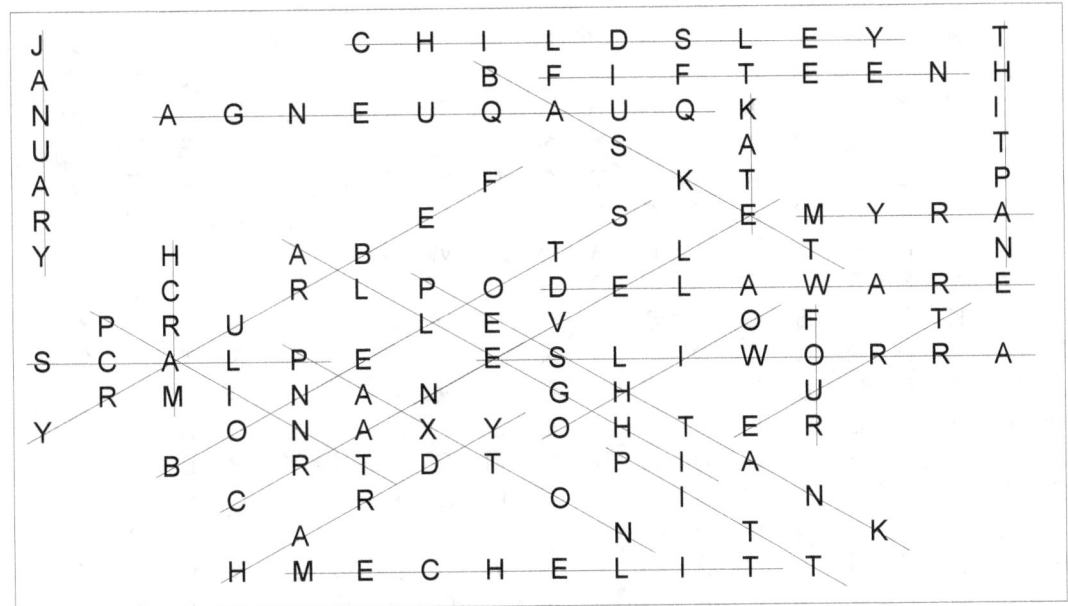

A Shawano who went on the raid with Thitpan: Cheek ___ (4)
Bejance's occupation: ___ maker (6)
Captured at 4 years of age & raised as an Indian: ___ Son (4)
Cousin who accompanied True Son on his journeys: Half ___ (5)
Dr. who thought True Son's illness was due to miasmas and captivity (9)
Fort at western end of the white settlements (4)
Indian language True Son spoke (8)
Indian name for Paxton (8)
Interpreter and guard: Del ___ (5)
Johnny's age when he was taken by the Indians (4)
Little Crane's brother who wanted to war against the whites (7)
Number of years John Butler lived with the Indians (6)
River where the boys stole the boat: ___ Sipu (7)
State in which the Tuscarawas River is located (4)
Tattooed warrior who went on the raid: Put-On-___ (5)
The Month When the First Frog Croaks (8)
The Month When the Ground Squirrels Begin to Run (7)
The Month of the Shad (5)
Thitpan had one that belonged to a white child (5)
Took True Son's Indian clothes away from him: Aunt ___ (4)
Township where True Son was born and massacre took place (6)
True Son and Half Arrrow's transportation down Ohio River: ___ boat (6)
True Son's Indian mother (9)
True Son's age at the beginning of the story (7)
True Son's older sister (8)
True Son's white mother (4)
Uncle leader of Paxton boys; killed & scalped Little Crane (5)
Was killed and scalped by Uncle Wilse: Little ___ (5)

Light in the Forest Word Search 3

```
S A P P L E C J B P M A R R O W T N S G
T L T A E N N A O L A Y K Y G I R O I P
O L H X N Y X N D H A R R X Y L U V S D
L E I T N P R U M X N C S A P S E E T S
E G T O I Q K A C T P M K O B E H M E Q
N H P N L R S R O C V U O P N C Z B R T
Z I A N R S T Y N A H S W H R S Y E T R
T Y N S A U Z C E P R K M A I M E R T Y
P K C Y S B Y S T I M E D O N W X K
M D R H R Q O D T A R N Z S C P G T A G
J E Z E P U N R O I E G R C L H U T Z W
N E V E L E E A G N E U Q A U Q E N T Y
D E C L E H S H O V O M G L N K R L T V
F Q I T B A L H A F M U B P S O A E I J
J H F Q A N H R T O E G X A C L W C P T
H I D G N N G P G A W Y B L C R A N E R
F A C P K A X A J G N E Q E F Z L A K Z
N S R M V N T I D T D K N C P S E J C Z
Z S L R R X B N M X Y T Q S C F D E L V
J Y T V Y R E T H C I R Y R A U R B E F
```

ALEC	DELAWARE	LENNI	PITT
ALLEGHI	ELEVEN	MARCH	PLAGUE
APPLE	FEBRUARY	MASSACRE	QUAQUENGA
ARROW	FEVER	MECHELIT	RICHTER
BANK	FIFTEEN	MUSKINGUM	SCALP
BASKET	FOUR	MYRA	SISTER
BEJANCE	GRAVE	NOVEMBER	STOLEN
BLACK	HARDY	OHIO	SUSQUEHANNA
BONE	HARRY	OWENS	THITPAN
CAPTAIN	HILL	PAINT	TREE
CONESTOGO	JANUARY	PARSON	TRUE
CORN	JOHN	PAXTON	WILSE
CRANE	KATE	PESHTANK	YENGUE

Light in the Forest Word Search 3 Answer Key

```
S  A     P  P  L  E     J     B  P  M  A  R  R  O  W     T  N     S
T  L     A  E           A     O  L  A        R            R  O     I
O  L     T  N           N     H  A  R        S            U  V     S
L  E     X  N           U     N  N  C        K            E  E     T
E  G     T  I           A        M  O        O            H  M     E
N  H     O              R        U  H        N            Y  B     R
   I     N              Y  S     S  M     M        C      E  E
         P                 U     K  A     E        P      N  R
         A              C  S  B  I  T     S        H      G     K
         N              R  Q  O  D  R     C        U      U     A
      E                 E  U  N  R  E     R        Q      E     T
   N  E  V  E  L  E  E  S  H  O  G  U  A  U  Q  K  R     N  T
      E        L  E                 O  M     L  P  S  O  A  E  I
   F  I  T     E  B              P  V     U     A     W  C  P  T
      H  F     A  A        H  A  R  O  E     B  C     R     A     
   H  I        N  N        P  I  T  W        L  C     A     N    
   F  A        K  K        A  N  N  E                        J   
              R                P           K        S       B  E  F
              R  Y  R  E  T  H  C  I  R  Y  R  A  U  R  B  E  F
```

ALEC	DELAWARE	LENNI	PITT
ALLEGHI	ELEVEN	MARCH	PLAGUE
APPLE	FEBRUARY	MASSACRE	QUAQUENGA
ARROW	FEVER	MECHELIT	RICHTER
BANK	FIFTEEN	MUSKINGUM	SCALP
BASKET	FOUR	MYRA	SISTER
BEJANCE	GRAVE	NOVEMBER	STOLEN
BLACK	HARDY	OHIO	SUSQUEHANNA
BONE	HARRY	OWENS	THITPAN
CAPTAIN	HILL	PAINT	TREE
CONESTOGO	JANUARY	PARSON	TRUE
CORN	JOHN	PAXTON	WILSE
CRANE	KATE	PESHTANK	YENGUE

Light in the Forest Word Search 4

```
D H M E C H E L I T G B S I S T E R P J
E Z Y G W C I D S H U L U N M R E Y E D
L N E V E L E L C T E K S A B U T A S H
A W R L R E V R L A O F Q C G E A R H C
W N A U R D A E T O J L U N A J K R T L
A M O T M M R V L B C O E N H L K O A C
R F F P L A G U E T J Y H N A C P W N F
E T E T A J S S C A J J A N R U A I K S
Y H B V K I L S N L H Q N A D Y R W T G
P I R V E I N U A F J M N F Y L S R O T
J T U W W R A T J C A E A K J O O O H T
Z P A M P R H Q E W R L A F K G N G I D
L A R Z Y H Q A B O R E L P I A T O O F
Z N Y R W R N C R E W I L E P F W T V N
X M D W S Q A B B R B E C G G L T S Z F
B X B Y B P G M L W Y A N H K H E E P P
B O N E T B E X E L G R N S T Y I N E Q
L F D A W V L T N B L A C K H E C O R B
T D I Q O L A G N E U Q A U Q R R C J J
T N B N X R M R I W K P P A X T O N Z H
                                        L
```

ALEC	CUYLOGA	KATE	PLAGUE
ALLEGHI	DELAWARE	LENNI	QUAQUENGA
APPLE	ELEVEN	MARCH	RICHTER
ARROW	FEBRUARY	MASSACRE	SCALP
BANK	FEVER	MECHELIT	SISTER
BASKET	FIFTEEN	MYRA	STOLEN
BEJANCE	FLATBOAT	NOVEMBER	SUSQUEHANNA
BLACK	FOUR	OHIO	THITPAN
BONE	GRAVE	OWENS	TREE
BUTLER	HARDY	PAINT	TRUE
CAPTAIN	HARRY	PARSON	WILSE
CONESTOGO	HILL	PAXTON	YENGUE
CORN	JANUARY	PESHTANK	
CRANE	JOHN	PITT	

Light in the Forest Word Search 4 Answer Key

ALEC	CUYLOGA	KATE	PLAGUE
ALLEGHI	DELAWARE	LENNI	QUAQUENGA
APPLE	ELEVEN	MARCH	RICHTER
ARROW	FEBRUARY	MASSACRE	SCALP
BANK	FEVER	MECHELIT	SISTER
BASKET	FIFTEEN	MYRA	STOLEN
BEJANCE	FLATBOAT	NOVEMBER	SUSQUEHANNA
BLACK	FOUR	OHIO	THITPAN
BONE	GRAVE	OWENS	TREE
BUTLER	HARDY	PAINT	TRUE
CAPTAIN	HARRY	PARSON	WILSE
CONESTOGO	HILL	PAXTON	YENGUE
CORN	JANUARY	PESHTANK	
CRANE	JOHN	PITT	

Light in the Forest Crossword 1

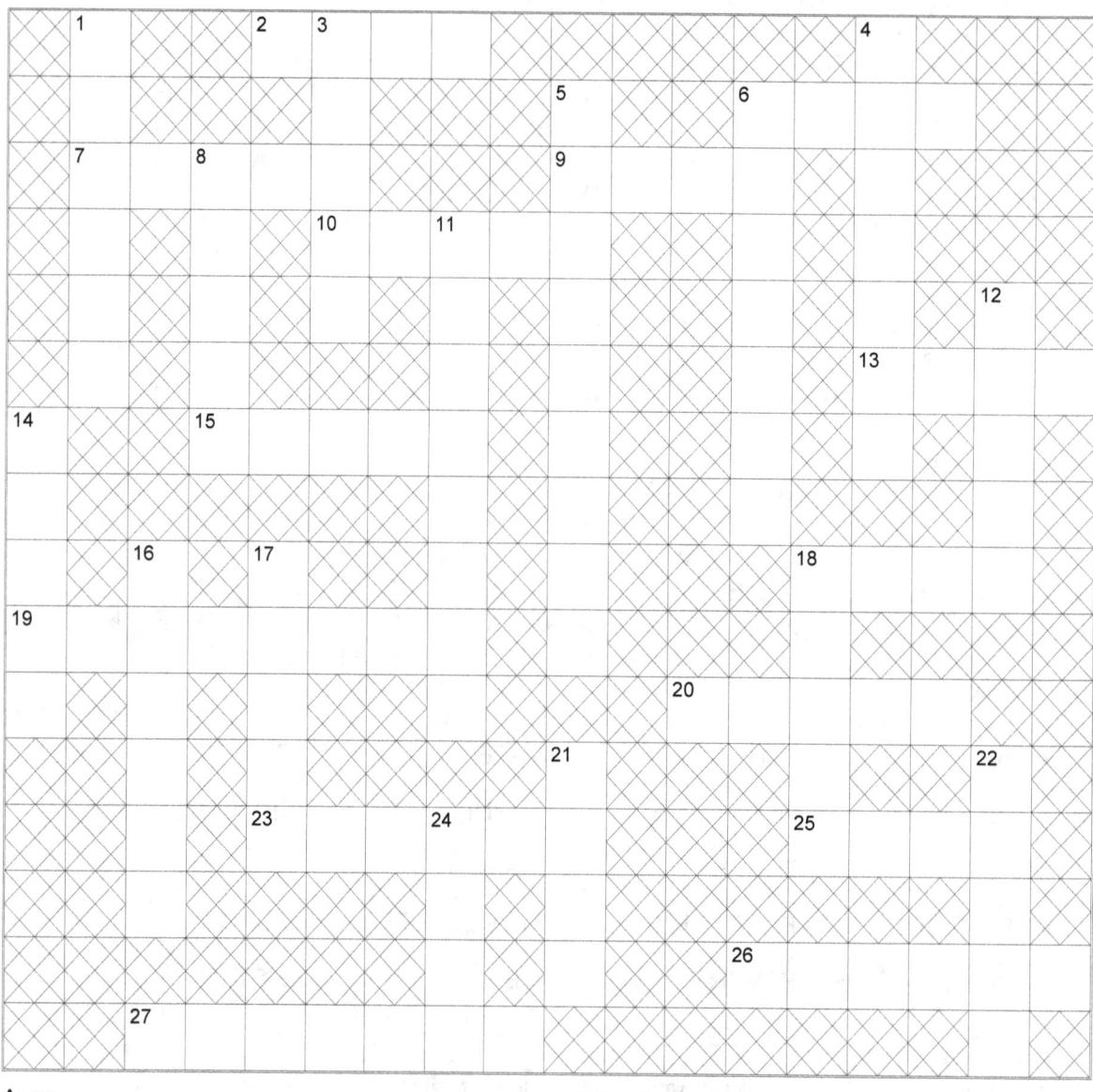

Across
2. Thitpan's father-in-law who had only one eye: High-___
6. Cousin who gave his white man's clothes to True Son
7. Thitpan had one that belonged to a white child
9. Under-The-___ put white clay on half of True Son's face
10. Tribe True Son belonged to: ___ Lenape
13. Indian rumored to live in the hills: ___ Blade
15. Uncle leader of Paxton boys; killed & scalped Little Crane
18. A Shawano who went on the raid with Thitpan: Cheek ___
19. Indian language True Son spoke
20. True Son thought sleeping in a bed in a house was like this
23. A'astonah was True Son's younger ___
25. Took True Son's Indian clothes away from him: Aunt ___
26. Wanted to wear True Son's Indian clothes: Gordie ___
27. True Son's age at the beginning of the story

Down
1. Bejance's occupation: ___ maker
3. True Son wanted to eat it to commit suicide: May ___
4. Negro slave and basket maker
5. Dr. who thought True Son's illness was due to miasmas and captivity
6. River where the boys stole the boat: ___ Sipu
8. Cousin who accompanied True Son on his journeys: Half ___
11. The Month of the First Snow
12. Was killed and scalped by Uncle Wilse: Little ___
14. Interpreter and guard: Del ___
16. Number of years John Butler lived with the Indians
17. Uncle George ___ tried to explain frontier justice to True Son
18. Half Arrow's father: ___ Fish
21. Captured at 4 years of age & raised as an Indian: ___ Son
22. True Son's illness caused by his captivity with whites
24. Where True Son hid when he heard he was to return to the whites

Light in the Forest Crossword 1 Answer Key

Grid solution (by clue number):

- 1 Down: BASKET
- 2 Across: BANK
- 3 Down: APPLE
- 4 Down: BUTLER
- 5 Down: CHILDS
- 6 Across: ALEC
- 6 Down: ALLEGHENY
- 7 Across: SCALP
- 8 Down: CARROT
- 9 Across: HILL
- 10 Across: LENNI
- 11 Down: NOVEMBER
- 12 Down: CRANE
- 13 Across: CORN
- 14 Down: HARRY
- 15 Across: WILSE
- 15 Down: WILEVEN (W-I-L-S-E-M-E-E-N-V-E-N)
- 16 Down: ELEVEN
- 17 Down: OWEN
- 18 Across: BONE
- 18 Down: BOLE
- 19 Across: DELAWARE
- 20 Across: GRAVE
- 21 Down: TRUE
- 22 Down: FEVER
- 23 Across: SISTER
- 24 Down: RRRE
- 25 Across: KATE
- 26 Across: BUTLER
- 27 Across: FIFTEEN

Across

2. Thitpan's father-in-law who had only one eye: High-___
6. Cousin who gave his white man's clothes to True Son
7. Thitpan had one that belonged to a white child
9. Under-The-___ put white clay on half of True Son's face
10. Tribe True Son belonged to: ___ Lenape
13. Indian rumored to live in the hills: ___ Blade
15. Uncle leader of Paxton boys; killed & scalped Little Crane
18. A Shawano who went on the raid with Thitpan: Cheek ___
19. Indian language True Son spoke
20. True Son thought sleeping in a bed in a house was like this
23. A'astonah was True Son's younger ___
25. Took True Son's Indian clothes away from him: Aunt ___
26. Wanted to wear True Son's Indian clothes: Gordie ___
27. True Son's age at the beginning of the story

Down

1. Bejance's occupation: ___ maker
3. True Son wanted to eat it to commit suicide: May ___
4. Negro slave and basket maker
5. Dr. who thought True Son's illness was due to miasmas and captivity
6. River where the boys stole the boat: ___ Sipu
8. Cousin who accompanied True Son on his journeys: Half ___
11. The Month of the First Snow
12. Was killed and scalped by Uncle Wilse: Little ___
14. Interpreter and guard: Del ___
16. Number of years John Butler lived with the Indians
17. Uncle George ___ tried to explain frontier justice to True Son
18. Half Arrow's father: ___ Fish
21. Captured at 4 years of age & raised as an Indian: ___ Son
22. True Son's illness caused by his captivity with whites
24. Where True Son hid when he heard he was to return to the whites

Light in the Forest Crossword 2

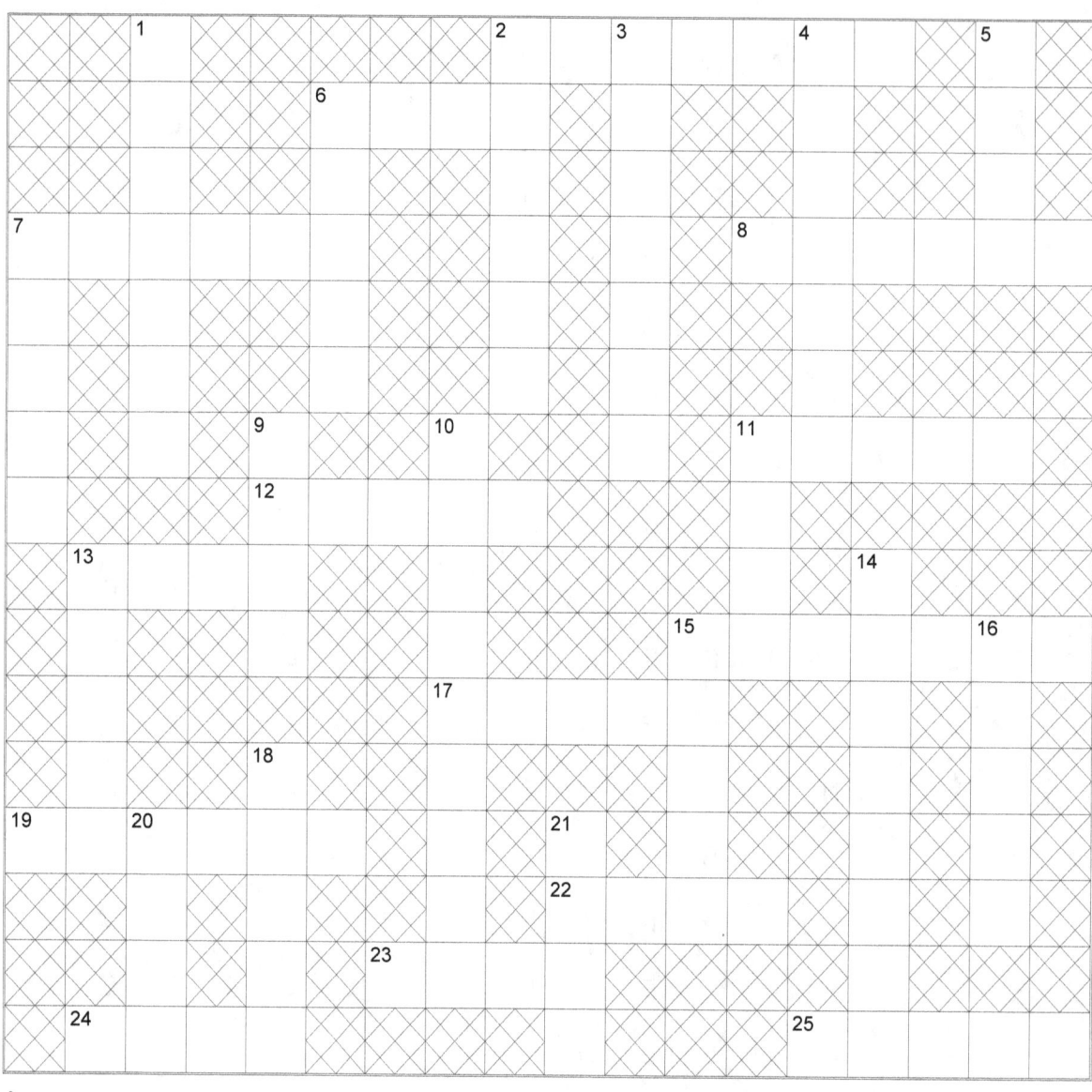

Across
2. Negro slave and basket maker
6. True Son's white mother
7. Wanted to wear True Son's Indian clothes: Gordie ___
8. Number of years John Butler lived with the Indians
11. Interpreter and guard: Del ___
12. Cousin who accompanied True Son on his journeys: Half ___
13. Fort at western end of the white settlements
15. River where the boys stole the boat: ___ Sipu
17. Thitpan had one that belonged to a white child
19. True Son and Half Arrrow's transportation down Ohio River: ___ boat
22. Cousin who gave his white man's clothes to True Son
23. Indian rumored to live in the hills: ___ Blade
24. Johnny's age when he was taken by the Indians
25. Tribe True Son belonged to: ___ Lenape

Down
1. Parson Elder's rank with the Paxton boys
2. Bejance's occupation: ___ maker
3. The Month When the Ground Squirrels Begin to Run
4. True Son's Indian father
5. A Shawano who went on the raid with Thitpan: Cheek ___
6. The Month of the Shad
7. Half Arrow's father: ___ Fish
9. Took True Son's Indian clothes away from him: Aunt ___
10. Tribe of Indians massacred at Peshtank
11. Under-The-___ put white clay on half of True Son's face
13. Tattooed warrior who went on the raid: Put-On-___
14. Indian language True Son spoke
15. True Son wanted to eat it to commit suicide: May ___
16. True Son's white father
18. True Son's illness caused by his captivity with whites
20. State in which the Tuscarawas River is located
21. Thitpan's father-in-law who had only one eye: High-___

Light in the Forest Crossword 2 Answer Key

	1 C			2 B	3 E	J	A	4 N	C	E	5 B	
	A		6 M	Y	R	A		A		U		O
	P			A		S		N		Y		N
7 B	U	T	L	E	R		K	U		8 E	L	E	V	E	N
L		A		C			E		A		O	
A		I		H			T		R		G	
C		N	9 K		10 C		Y		11 H	A	R	D	Y
K			12 A	R	R	O	W		I			
	13 P	I	T	T		N			L		14 D	
	A			E			15 A	L	L	E	G	H	16 I
	I				17 S	C	A	L	P		L		A
	N		18 F		T			P		A		R
19 S	20 T	O	L	E	N		21 B		L			W	R
	H		V			G		22 A	L	E	C		A	Y
	I		E		23 C	O	R	N				R
	24 F	O	U	R			K		25 L	E	N	N	I

Across
2. Negro slave and basket maker
6. True Son's white mother
7. Wanted to wear True Son's Indian clothes: Gordie ___
8. Number of years John Butler lived with the Indians
11. Interpreter and guard: Del ___
12. Cousin who accompanied True Son on his journeys: Half ___
13. Fort at western end of the white settlements
15. River where the boys stole the boat: ___ Sipu
17. Thitpan had one that belonged to a white child
19. True Son and Half Arrrow's transportation down Ohio River: ___ boat
22. Cousin who gave his white man's clothes to True Son
23. Indian rumored to live in the hills: ___ Blade
24. Johnny's age when he was taken by the Indians
25. Tribe True Son belonged to: ___ Lenape

Down
1. Parson Elder's rank with the Paxton boys
2. Bejance's occupation: ___ maker
3. The Month When the Ground Squirrels Begin to Run
4. True Son's Indian father
5. A Shawano who went on the raid with Thitpan: Cheek ___
6. The Month of the Shad
7. Half Arrow's father: ___ Fish
9. Took True Son's Indian clothes away from him: Aunt ___
10. Tribe of Indians massacred at Peshtank
11. Under-The-___ put white clay on half of True Son's face
13. Tattooed warrior who went on the raid: Put-On-___
14. Indian language True Son spoke
15. True Son wanted to eat it to commit suicide: May ___
16. True Son's white father
18. True Son's illness caused by his captivity with whites
20. State in which the Tuscarawas River is located
21. Thitpan's father-in-law who had only one eye: High-___

Light in the Forest Crossword 3

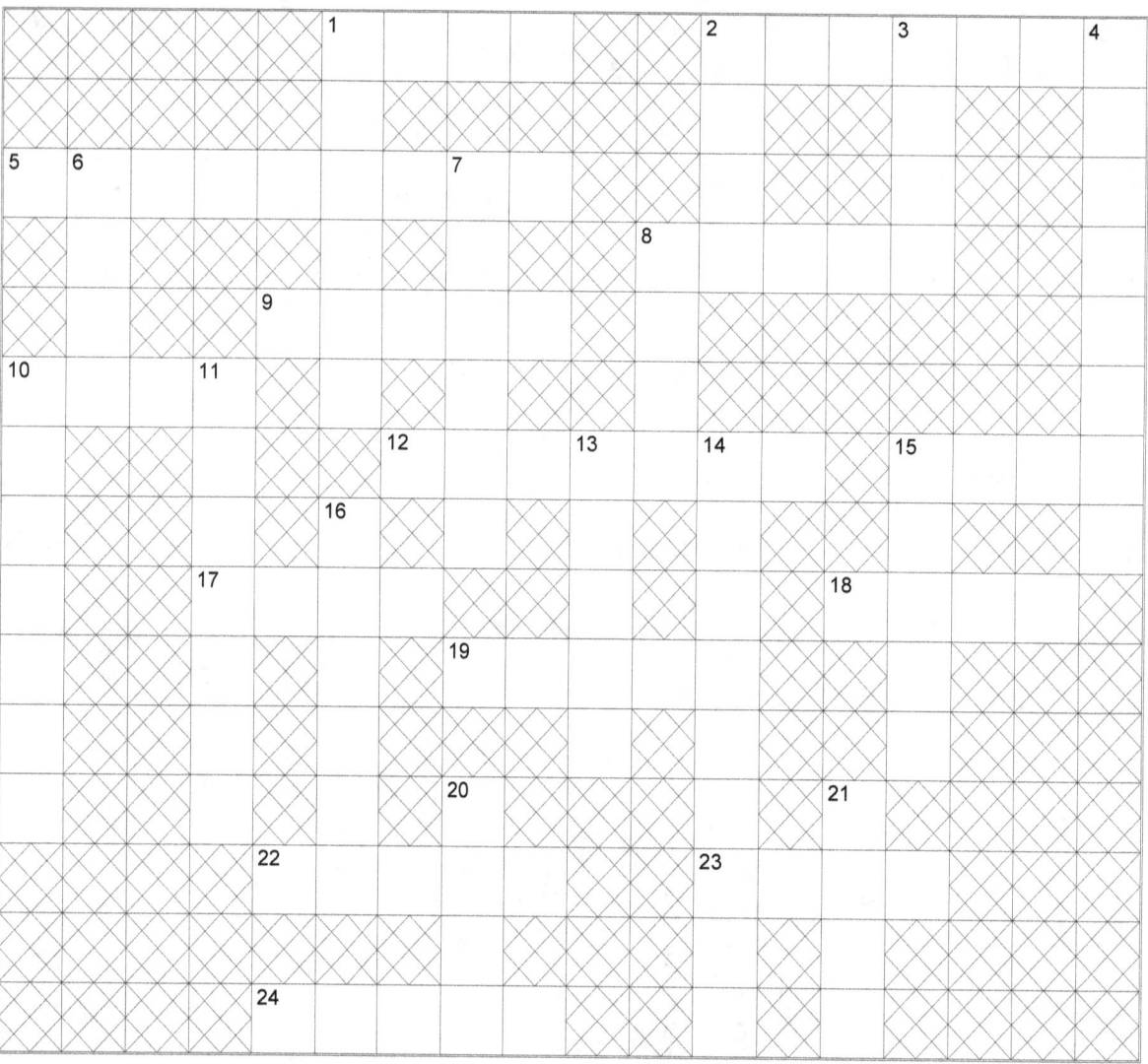

Across
1. Thitpan's father-in-law who had only one eye: High-___
2. True Son's age at the beginning of the story
5. Dr. who thought True Son's illness was due to miasmas and captivity
8. Was killed and scalped by Uncle Wilse: Little ___
9. True Son's illness caused by his captivity with whites
10. Cousin who gave his white man's clothes to True Son
12. Negro slave and basket maker
15. A Shawano who went on the raid with Thitpan: Cheek ___
17. Captured at 4 years of age & raised as an Indian: ___ Son
18. Took True Son's Indian clothes away from him: Aunt ___
19. Uncle leader of Paxton boys; killed & scalped Little Crane
22. Cousin who accompanied True Son on his journeys: Half ___
23. State in which the Tuscarawas River is located
24. Tribe True Son belonged to: ___ Lenape

Down
1. Bejance's occupation: ___ maker
2. Johnny's age when he was taken by the Indians
3. Where True Son hid when he heard he was to return to the whites
4. The Month of the First Snow
6. Under-The-___ put white clay on half of True Son's face
7. Number of years John Butler lived with the Indians
8. Indian rumored to live in the hills: ___ Blade
10. River where the boys stole the boat: ___ Sipu
11. Parson Elder's rank with the Paxton boys
13. True Son wanted to eat it to commit suicide: May ___
14. Tribe of Indians massacred at Peshtank
15. Half Arrow's father: ___ Fish
16. Wanted to wear True Son's Indian clothes: Gordie ___
20. True Son's white name: ___ Cameron Butler
21. Fort at western end of the white settlements

Light in the Forest Crossword 3 Answer Key

				1 B	A	N	K		2 F	I	3 F	T	E	E	4 N
				A					O		R				O
5 C	6 H	I	L	D	S	7 L	E	Y			E				V
	I			K		L			8 C	R	A	N	E		E
	L		9 F	E	V	E	R		O						M
10 A	L	11 E	T			V			R						B
L		C	A		12 B	E	J	13 A	N	14 C	E		15 B	O	N	E
L		A		16 B	N		P		O			L		R
E		17 T	R	U	E		P		N		18 K	A	T	E
G		A		T		19 W	I	L	S	E		C		
H		I		L				E		S		K		
I		N		E		20 J				T		21 P		
			22 A	R	R	O	W		23 O	H	I	O		
						H			G			T		
			24 L	E	N	N	I		O			T		

Across
1. Thitpan's father-in-law who had only one eye: High-___
2. True Son's age at the beginning of the story
5. Dr. who thought True Son's illness was due to miasmas and captivity
8. Was killed and scalped by Uncle Wilse: Little ___
9. True Son's illness caused by his captivity with whites
10. Cousin who gave his white man's clothes to True Son
12. Negro slave and basket maker
15. A Shawano who went on the raid with Thitpan: Cheek ___
17. Captured at 4 years of age & raised as an Indian: ___ Son
18. Took True Son's Indian clothes away from him: Aunt ___
19. Uncle leader of Paxton boys; killed & scalped Little Crane
22. Cousin who accompanied True Son on his journeys: Half ___
23. State in which the Tuscarawas River is located
24. Tribe True Son belonged to: ___ Lenape

Down
1. Bejance's occupation: ___ maker
2. Johnny's age when he was taken by the Indians
3. Where True Son hid when he heard he was to return to the whites
4. The Month of the First Snow
6. Under-The-___ put white clay on half of True Son's face
7. Number of years John Butler lived with the Indians
8. Indian rumored to live in the hills: ___ Blade
10. River where the boys stole the boat: ___ Sipu
11. Parson Elder's rank with the Paxton boys
13. True Son wanted to eat it to commit suicide: May ___
14. Tribe of Indians massacred at Peshtank
15. Half Arrow's father: ___ Fish
16. Wanted to wear True Son's Indian clothes: Gordie ___
20. True Son's white name: ___ Cameron Butler
21. Fort at western end of the white settlements

Light in the Forest Crossword 4

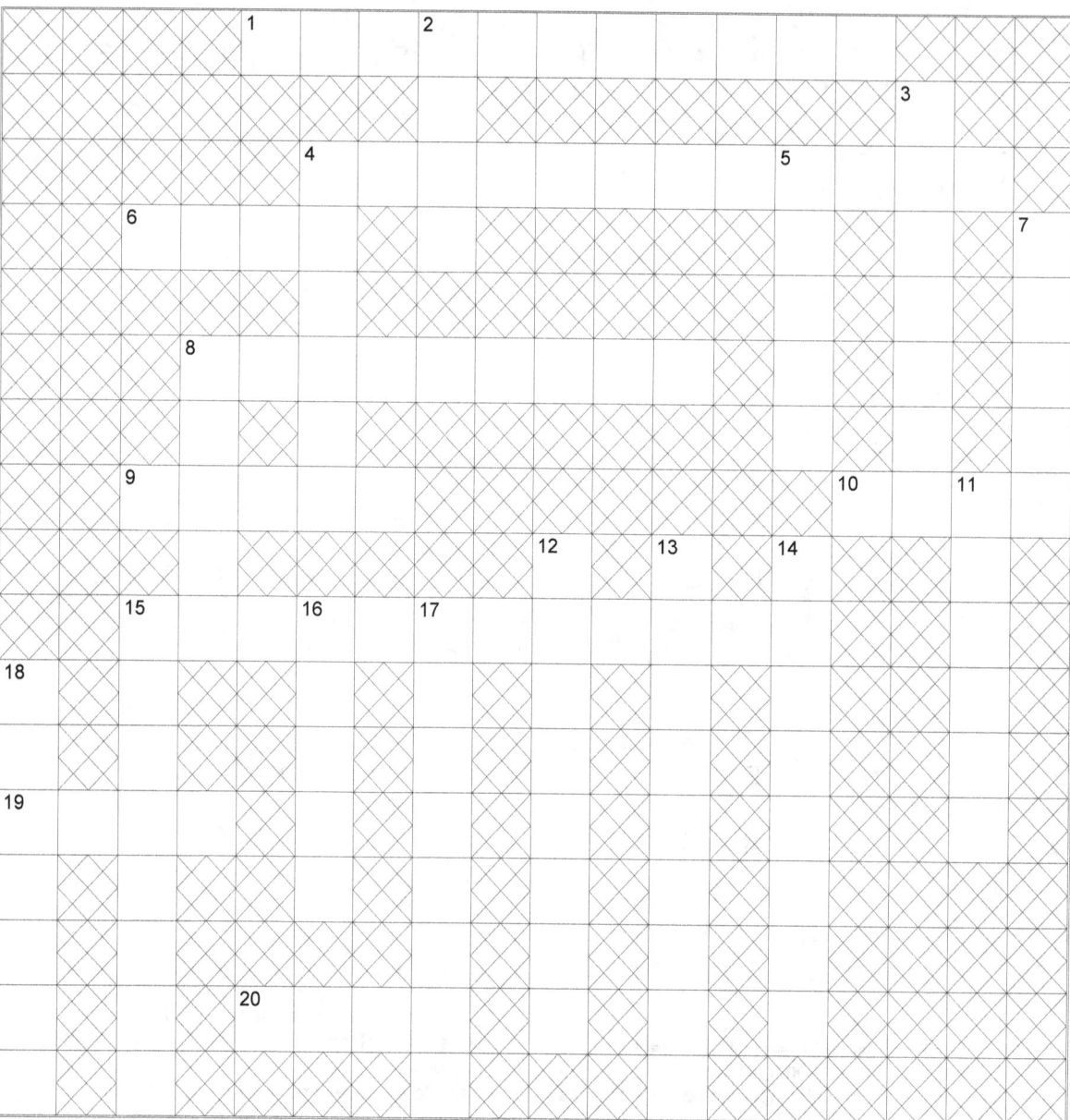

Across
1. Blackened half of True Son's face
4. Location of Fort Pitt and Paxton Township
6. True Son's white mother
8. River where the boys bathed when they returned to their tribe
9. Was killed and scalped by Uncle Wilse: Little ___
10. Where True Son hid when he heard he was to return to the whites
15. City where Indians received sympathetic treatment
19. True Son's white name: ___ Cameron Butler
20. Johnny's age when he was taken by the Indians

Down
2. Thitpan's father-in-law who had only one eye: High-___
3. Author
4. Peshtank captain; sacrificed Indian lives to save his favorite horse: ___ Elder
5. Cousin who accompanied True Son on his journeys: Half ___
7. True Son thought sleeping in a bed in a house was like this
8. The Month of the Shad
11. Number of years John Butler lived with the Indians
12. True Son warned its occupants of an ambush
13. Dr. who thought True Son's illness was due to miasmas and captivity
14. What the Paxton boys did to the Conestogo Indians
15. Indian name for Paxton
16. Tribe True Son belonged to: ___ Lenape
17. Indian language True Son spoke
18. Negro slave and basket maker

Light in the Forest Crossword 4 Answer Key

			1 D	I	2 S	B	E	L	I	E	V	E	R		
					A								3 R		
			4 P	E	N	N	S	Y	L	V	5 A	N	I	A	
	6 M	Y	R	A	K						R		C		7 G
			R								R		H		R
		8 M	U	S	K	I	N	G	U	M	O		T		A
		A		O							W		E		V
		9 C	R	A	N	E			12		10 T	11 R	E	E
		C					12 F		13 C		14 M		L		
	15 P	H	I	16 L	A	17 D	E	L	P	H	I	A		E	
18 B	E			E		E		A		I		S		V	
E	S			N		N		T		L		S		E	
19 J	O	H	N		N		A		B		D		A		N
A	T			I			W		O		S		C		
N	A						A		A		L		R		
C	N		20 F	O	U	R			T		E		E		
E	K					E					Y				

Across
1. Blackened half of True Son's face
4. Location of Fort Pitt and Paxton Township
6. True Son's white mother
8. River where the boys bathed when they returned to their tribe
9. Was killed and scalped by Uncle Wilse: Little ___
10. Where True Son hid when he heard he was to return to the whites
15. City where Indians received sympathetic treatment
19. True Son's white name: ___ Cameron Butler
20. Johnny's age when he was taken by the Indians

Down
2. Thitpan's father-in-law who had only one eye: High-___
3. Author
4. Peshtank captain; sacrificed Indian lives to save his favorite horse: ___ Elder
5. Cousin who accompanied True Son on his journeys: Half ___
7. True Son thought sleeping in a bed in a house was like this
8. The Month of the Shad
11. Number of years John Butler lived with the Indians
12. True Son warned its occupants of an ambush
13. Dr. who thought True Son's illness was due to miasmas and captivity
14. What the Paxton boys did to the Conestogo Indians
15. Indian name for Paxton
16. Tribe True Son belonged to: ___ Lenape
17. Indian language True Son spoke
18. Negro slave and basket maker

Light in the Forest

ELEVEN	FIFTEEN	ARROW	JANUARY	HILL
PARSON	HARRY	PESHTANK	CRANE	OWENS
FOUR	DISBELIEVER	FREE SPACE	YENGUE	WILSE
NOVEMBER	ALEC	MUSKINGUM	TRUE	CORN
CUYLOGA	PLAGUE	QUAQUENGA	FLATBOAT	BUTLER

Light in the Forest

GRAVE	BLACK	STOLEN	SISTER	PAXTON
FEBRUARY	APPLE	PHILADELPHIA	SUSQUEHANNA	BASKET
OHIO	THITPAN	FREE SPACE	BANK	RICHTER
BONE	HARDY	KATE	PAINT	TREE
DELAWARE	SCALP	FEVER	CAPTAIN	MARCH

Light in the Forest

NOVEMBER	SUSQUEHANNA	BONE	CAPTAIN	BEJANCE
BLACK	WILSE	FIFTEEN	APPLE	PENNSYLVANIA
ALLEGHI	FEBRUARY	FREE SPACE	PARSON	CORN
TREE	QUAQUENGA	PAINT	PITT	JOHN
FOUR	PESHTANK	MECHELIT	YENGUE	TUSCARAWAS

Light in the Forest

ELEVEN	BANK	PAXTON	TRUE	OWENS
CRANE	HARDY	FLATBOAT	HILL	PHILADELPHIA
MASSACRE	DISBELIEVER	FREE SPACE	THITPAN	SISTER
MARCH	LENNI	RICHTER	BASKET	STOLEN
JANUARY	MUSKINGUM	SCALP	CUYLOGA	CONESTOGO

Light in the Forest

CHILDSLEY	APPLE	MUSKINGUM	PHILADELPHIA	LENNI
CRANE	CORN	PARSON	PENNSYLVANIA	ELEVEN
PLAGUE	BANK	FREE SPACE	FEVER	STOLEN
ARROW	JANUARY	BASKET	KATE	NOVEMBER
BUTLER	FOUR	FEBRUARY	ALLEGHI	CUYLOGA

Light in the Forest

MYRA	PESHTANK	FIFTEEN	SISTER	RICHTER
OHIO	BONE	SUSQUEHANNA	ALEC	PAXTON
PAINT	OWENS	FREE SPACE	JOHN	THITPAN
HARDY	DISBELIEVER	MARCH	WILSE	BLACK
TUSCARAWAS	TRUE	YENGUE	MECHELIT	QUAQUENGA

Light in the Forest

CHILDSLEY	NOVEMBER	LENNI	PENNSYLVANIA	MYRA
TREE	PLAGUE	FLATBOAT	SCALP	MARCH
WILSE	DISBELIEVER	FREE SPACE	BLACK	HARDY
CAPTAIN	FEBRUARY	HARRY	PARSON	BASKET
PAXTON	APPLE	PAINT	YENGUE	PITT

Light in the Forest

PHILADELPHIA	TUSCARAWAS	FIFTEEN	DELAWARE	MASSACRE
KATE	SISTER	FOUR	CONESTOGO	BONE
MECHELIT	OHIO	FREE SPACE	ALLEGHI	JANUARY
CORN	BEJANCE	STOLEN	CUYLOGA	ARROW
HILL	MUSKINGUM	THITPAN	FEVER	TRUE

Light in the Forest

TRUE	DELAWARE	HARDY	PLAGUE	PARSON
CHILDSLEY	ALLEGHI	ARROW	FOUR	MYRA
OHIO	CAPTAIN	FREE SPACE	BANK	SCALP
ALEC	FEVER	CONESTOGO	CRANE	PAXTON
PESHTANK	YENGUE	BASKET	FIFTEEN	DISBELIEVER

Light in the Forest

WILSE	BEJANCE	STOLEN	NOVEMBER	QUAQUENGA
BONE	CORN	CUYLOGA	HILL	FLATBOAT
MECHELIT	PHILADELPHIA	FREE SPACE	BLACK	OWENS
SISTER	MARCH	MUSKINGUM	KATE	LENNI
ELEVEN	SUSQUEHANNA	TREE	RICHTER	PAINT

Light in the Forest

FEBRUARY	YENGUE	PAXTON	BASKET	MASSACRE
MYRA	DELAWARE	GRAVE	PITT	ALEC
SUSQUEHANNA	PENNSYLVANIA	FREE SPACE	MECHELIT	CRANE
QUAQUENGA	KATE	NOVEMBER	FLATBOAT	JOHN
SCALP	PLAGUE	TRUE	RICHTER	MARCH

Light in the Forest

CUYLOGA	BLACK	BONE	CAPTAIN	MUSKINGUM
DISBELIEVER	WILSE	PAINT	FIFTEEN	CORN
ELEVEN	TUSCARAWAS	FREE SPACE	OHIO	SISTER
FOUR	STOLEN	CHILDSLEY	BANK	OWENS
LENNI	HILL	PHILADELPHIA	JANUARY	CONESTOGO

Light in the Forest

SUSQUEHANNA	KATE	PENNSYLVANIA	BASKET	FOUR
BONE	PAINT	SISTER	PHILADELPHIA	BUTLER
ALEC	FIFTEEN	FREE SPACE	MECHELIT	THITPAN
FEVER	BANK	PAXTON	NOVEMBER	WILSE
CHILDSLEY	CAPTAIN	CONESTOGO	CORN	LENNI

Light in the Forest

CUYLOGA	ARROW	STOLEN	FLATBOAT	JOHN
MASSACRE	OHIO	HILL	JANUARY	TRUE
PESHTANK	CRANE	FREE SPACE	PARSON	MYRA
BEJANCE	DELAWARE	QUAQUENGA	TREE	MUSKINGUM
ALLEGHI	DISBELIEVER	APPLE	ELEVEN	FEBRUARY

Light in the Forest

ELEVEN	MYRA	OWENS	SISTER	NOVEMBER
CONESTOGO	TUSCARAWAS	TRUE	MASSACRE	ALLEGHI
FIFTEEN	PARSON	FREE SPACE	MECHELIT	CAPTAIN
HARRY	BUTLER	YENGUE	PAXTON	JOHN
PESHTANK	JANUARY	STOLEN	MUSKINGUM	GRAVE

Light in the Forest

THITPAN	SUSQUEHANNA	FEBRUARY	BEJANCE	QUAQUENGA
APPLE	PITT	TREE	PAINT	HILL
LENNI	PLAGUE	FREE SPACE	CHILDSLEY	BLACK
PHILADELPHIA	KATE	HARDY	WILSE	CRANE
FOUR	ARROW	OHIO	PENNSYLVANIA	CORN

Light in the Forest

BLACK	CORN	PARSON	LENNI	FLATBOAT
BUTLER	CHILDSLEY	PITT	PENNSYLVANIA	SCALP
OWENS	WILSE	FREE SPACE	FEVER	THITPAN
MYRA	ALEC	PESHTANK	ALLEGHI	STOLEN
HARRY	PLAGUE	FEBRUARY	BONE	CRANE

Light in the Forest

PHILADELPHIA	DISBELIEVER	TREE	FIFTEEN	KATE
RICHTER	ELEVEN	MUSKINGUM	SISTER	SUSQUEHANNA
HILL	FOUR	FREE SPACE	JOHN	MECHELIT
HARDY	BANK	JANUARY	MARCH	BASKET
PAINT	NOVEMBER	TRUE	CONESTOGO	PAXTON

Light in the Forest

YENGUE	CRANE	PENNSYLVANIA	STOLEN	PITT
HARRY	SUSQUEHANNA	PAXTON	FEVER	APPLE
MECHELIT	JANUARY	FREE SPACE	OHIO	PARSON
MYRA	RICHTER	KATE	BEJANCE	FIFTEEN
MASSACRE	FOUR	LENNI	BASKET	JOHN

Light in the Forest

ALLEGHI	MUSKINGUM	FLATBOAT	BUTLER	GRAVE
SCALP	ARROW	MARCH	HILL	CUYLOGA
THITPAN	BLACK	FREE SPACE	TREE	NOVEMBER
PLAGUE	PAINT	PESHTANK	ALEC	CHILDSLEY
WILSE	CAPTAIN	ELEVEN	CORN	QUAQUENGA

Light in the Forest

PLAGUE	APPLE	FEVER	TUSCARAWAS	JOHN
WILSE	THITPAN	MECHELIT	MASSACRE	KATE
MARCH	HARRY	FREE SPACE	CHILDSLEY	YENGUE
DELAWARE	JANUARY	PAINT	PAXTON	RICHTER
PENNSYLVANIA	STOLEN	CORN	OHIO	PARSON

Light in the Forest

SUSQUEHANNA	HARDY	MYRA	OWENS	PESHTANK
BANK	ELEVEN	BLACK	ARROW	LENNI
ALLEGHI	BONE	FREE SPACE	BEJANCE	GRAVE
FEBRUARY	TRUE	BASKET	MUSKINGUM	SCALP
CUYLOGA	SISTER	HILL	BUTLER	CAPTAIN

Light in the Forest

ELEVEN	HILL	CRANE	MUSKINGUM	BONE
MYRA	BEJANCE	TREE	OHIO	PLAGUE
BLACK	BUTLER	FREE SPACE	CHILDSLEY	PARSON
FIFTEEN	PENNSYLVANIA	TUSCARAWAS	QUAQUENGA	PESHTANK
ALLEGHI	PHILADELPHIA	DISBELIEVER	ALEC	NOVEMBER

Light in the Forest

WILSE	MASSACRE	SUSQUEHANNA	CAPTAIN	JANUARY
KATE	FOUR	CORN	YENGUE	STOLEN
FEVER	FLATBOAT	FREE SPACE	PAINT	CUYLOGA
BASKET	SCALP	ARROW	THITPAN	GRAVE
FEBRUARY	RICHTER	MECHELIT	PITT	DELAWARE

Light in the Forest

BEJANCE	NOVEMBER	RICHTER	PARSON	TREE
HARRY	STOLEN	ARROW	QUAQUENGA	PESHTANK
JOHN	CAPTAIN	FREE SPACE	BUTLER	PENNSYLVANIA
HILL	MUSKINGUM	ELEVEN	SUSQUEHANNA	PAXTON
PHILADELPHIA	PITT	OWENS	APPLE	SCALP

Light in the Forest

SISTER	JANUARY	PLAGUE	MARCH	THITPAN
CHILDSLEY	WILSE	YENGUE	FLATBOAT	GRAVE
MASSACRE	BLACK	FREE SPACE	ALLEGHI	FOUR
TUSCARAWAS	FEBRUARY	BANK	FIFTEEN	LENNI
CRANE	CONESTOGO	BONE	DISBELIEVER	DELAWARE

Light in the Forest

CORN	DELAWARE	MYRA	CONESTOGO	MUSKINGUM
OWENS	PAINT	JOHN	DISBELIEVER	SCALP
PARSON	CAPTAIN	FREE SPACE	MECHELIT	SUSQUEHANNA
MARCH	SISTER	CUYLOGA	BANK	PESHTANK
FIFTEEN	HARDY	JANUARY	HARRY	BONE

Light in the Forest

ELEVEN	RICHTER	PENNSYLVANIA	TUSCARAWAS	OHIO
BUTLER	PLAGUE	CRANE	GRAVE	FOUR
ALEC	PAXTON	FREE SPACE	TREE	CHILDSLEY
QUAQUENGA	ALLEGHI	BEJANCE	NOVEMBER	THITPAN
LENNI	HILL	ARROW	FLATBOAT	TRUE

Light in the Forest

MASSACRE	MECHELIT	APPLE	HILL	FEVER
YENGUE	WILSE	BUTLER	ELEVEN	TRUE
JANUARY	DISBELIEVER	FREE SPACE	ALEC	STOLEN
SISTER	PHILADELPHIA	CONESTOGO	BLACK	PESHTANK
CORN	JOHN	RICHTER	CRANE	NOVEMBER

Light in the Forest

ARROW	PARSON	OWENS	CUYLOGA	ALLEGHI
PAINT	HARDY	PLAGUE	SCALP	TUSCARAWAS
BONE	CHILDSLEY	FREE SPACE	MUSKINGUM	FIFTEEN
HARRY	BANK	MYRA	CAPTAIN	SUSQUEHANNA
PITT	FEBRUARY	FLATBOAT	DELAWARE	QUAQUENGA

Light in the Forest

CAPTAIN	MASSACRE	GRAVE	TREE	FOUR
PARSON	LENNI	BANK	ALEC	APPLE
SUSQUEHANNA	JANUARY	FREE SPACE	CONESTOGO	KATE
MECHELIT	FEVER	BUTLER	SISTER	WILSE
BONE	HARDY	MARCH	CHILDSLEY	CORN

Light in the Forest

PAINT	CRANE	PENNSYLVANIA	PITT	OHIO
JOHN	PESHTANK	HARRY	SCALP	OWENS
ALLEGHI	PLAGUE	FREE SPACE	CUYLOGA	BEJANCE
TUSCARAWAS	DISBELIEVER	HILL	YENGUE	STOLEN
BLACK	ARROW	BASKET	QUAQUENGA	PAXTON

Light in the Forest Vocabulary Word List

No. Word	Clue/Definition
1. ABDUCTOR	Kidnapper
2. ABHORRENCE	A feeling of repugnance or loathing
3. ALACRITY	Speed or quickness
4. ALLOTTED	Distributed
5. ALOOFNESS	Distant physically or emotionally; reserved and remote
6. APPEASE	Pacify; soothe
7. ASSENTED	Agreed
8. AVERSION	A feeling of extreme repugnance accompanied by avoidance
9. BERATING	Scolding; belittling
10. BLEAKLY	Gloomily; without cheer
11. BUSTLE	Excited and often noisy activity
12. CONDONE	To overlook, forgive, or disregard without protest
13. CONSOLATION	Relieving the sorrow or grief
14. COUNSEL	Advice
15. COVET	To want something that belongs to another
16. DEBASED	Lowered in character, quality, or value; degraded
17. DEFIANT	Boldly resisting
18. DERISION	Ridicule
19. DESOLATE	Barren; lifeless
20. DESTINATION	The place to which one is going
21. DETERRED	Prevented or discouraged from acting
22. DISCERNED	Recognized or comprehended mentally
23. DISPOSITION	Temperament; usual mood
24. DISTORTED	Twisted; misshapen
25. DOUGHTIER	More courageous
26. ENCUMBRANCES	Burdens or obstacles
27. ENDURE	To suffer patiently without yielding
28. EXEMPLARY	Worthy of being imitated
29. EXERTION	Effort
30. EXULTATION	Rejoicing
31. FATHOM	Understand
32. FILIAL	Pertaining to a son or daughter
33. FORMIDABLE	Arousing fear, dread, or alarm
34. GRIMACE	A twisting of the face that expresses pain, contempt, or disgust
35. HEEDLESS	Not paying attention
36. HOVER	Hang about; wait nearby
37. HUMILIATING	Lowering the pride, dignity, or self-respect
38. IMPERIAL	Having supreme authority
39. INCREDULITY	Disbelief
40. INSIDIOUS	Intended to entrap; treacherous
41. LACKEYS	Slaves; forced laborers
42. LOATHING	Great dislike; abhorrence
43. MERIDIAN	Highest point; peak
44. MERITORIOUS	Deserving reward or praise
45. MIASMAS	Swamp gas; odor of decaying matter
46. MOLEST	To disturb, interfere with, or annoy
47. ODIOUS	Arousing strong dislike or intense displeasure
48. OMINOUS	Threatening
49. OSTENTATION	Boastful display meant to impress others; showiness
50. PALLID	Having an abnormally pale complexion
51. PESTILENCE	A destructive, evil influence
52. PRECEPTS	Rules or principles
53. PRESUMPTUOUS	Going beyond what is right or proper; excessively forward

Light in the Forest Vocabulary Word List

No.	Word	Clue/Definition
54.	PUNGENCY	Stinging; capable of burning
55.	PURGING	Purifying; cleansing
56.	REMONSTRATING	Pleading in protest
57.	REMUNERATION	Payment
58.	SAPLING	A young tree
59.	SEINE	Net for catching fish
60.	SINISTER	Evil
61.	SOLACE	Comfort in trouble
62.	SOMBER	Dark; gloomy
63.	STEALTHY	Acting with secrecy to avoid notice
64.	STOLID	Having or revealing little emotion
65.	SUBJUGATION	Act of bringing under control; conquering
66.	SUFFOCATING	Killing by taking away oxygen
67.	SULLEN	Brooding; morose; sulky
68.	TAINTED	Stained; infected; spoiled
69.	TRIBULATIONS	Great afflictions or suffering
70.	TRUSSED	Tied up
71.	VALOR	Courage; bravery
72.	VARMINT	One that is considered undesirable, obnoxious, or troublesome
73.	VERMILION	A vivid red to reddish orange
74.	VOLITION	A conscious choice or decision

Light in the Forest Vocabulary Fill In The Blank 1

_____ 1. To want something that belongs to another
_____ 2. A conscious choice or decision
_____ 3. To disturb, interfere with, or annoy
_____ 4. Deserving reward or praise
_____ 5. Purifying; cleansing
_____ 6. Worthy of being imitated
_____ 7. Advice
_____ 8. Threatening
_____ 9. Arousing strong dislike or intense displeasure
_____ 10. Great afflictions or suffering
_____ 11. Stinging; capable of burning
_____ 12. Temperament; usual mood
_____ 13. To suffer patiently without yielding
_____ 14. Barren; lifeless
_____ 15. A young tree
_____ 16. Having an abnormally pale complexion
_____ 17. Twisted; misshapen
_____ 18. Kidnapper
_____ 19. Distributed
_____ 20. Scolding; belittling

Light in the Forest Vocabulary Fill In The Blank 1 Answer Key

COVET	1. To want something that belongs to another
VOLITION	2. A conscious choice or decision
MOLEST	3. To disturb, interfere with, or annoy
MERITORIOUS	4. Deserving reward or praise
PURGING	5. Purifying; cleansing
EXEMPLARY	6. Worthy of being imitated
COUNSEL	7. Advice
OMINOUS	8. Threatening
ODIOUS	9. Arousing strong dislike or intense displeasure
TRIBULATIONS	10. Great afflictions or suffering
PUNGENCY	11. Stinging; capable of burning
DISPOSITION	12. Temperament; usual mood
ENDURE	13. To suffer patiently without yielding
DESOLATE	14. Barren; lifeless
SAPLING	15. A young tree
PALLID	16. Having an abnormally pale complexion
DISTORTED	17. Twisted; misshapen
ABDUCTOR	18. Kidnapper
ALLOTTED	19. Distributed
BERATING	20. Scolding; belittling

Light in the Forest Vocabulary Fill In The Blank 2

_____ 1. A young tree

_____ 2. Arousing fear, dread, or alarm

_____ 3. To disturb, interfere with, or annoy

_____ 4. Intended to entrap; treacherous

_____ 5. Comfort in trouble

_____ 6. Pacify; soothe

_____ 7. A feeling of repugnance or loathing

_____ 8. Barren; lifeless

_____ 9. Prevented or discouraged from acting

_____ 10. Stinging; capable of burning

_____ 11. Agreed

_____ 12. The place to which one is going

_____ 13. Great dislike; abhorrence

_____ 14. To want something that belongs to another

_____ 15. Rejoicing

_____ 16. Brooding; morose; sulky

_____ 17. Rules or principles

_____ 18. Disbelief

_____ 19. Killing by taking away oxygen

_____ 20. Going beyond what is right or proper; excessively forward

Light in the Forest Vocabulary Fill In The Blank 2 Answer Key

SAPLING	1. A young tree
FORMIDABLE	2. Arousing fear, dread, or alarm
MOLEST	3. To disturb, interfere with, or annoy
INSIDIOUS	4. Intended to entrap; treacherous
SOLACE	5. Comfort in trouble
APPEASE	6. Pacify; soothe
ABHORRENCE	7. A feeling of repugnance or loathing
DESOLATE	8. Barren; lifeless
DETERRED	9. Prevented or discouraged from acting
PUNGENCY	10. Stinging; capable of burning
ASSENTED	11. Agreed
DESTINATION	12. The place to which one is going
LOATHING	13. Great dislike; abhorrence
COVET	14. To want something that belongs to another
EXULTATION	15. Rejoicing
SULLEN	16. Brooding; morose; sulky
PRECEPTS	17. Rules or principles
INCREDULITY	18. Disbelief
SUFFOCATING	19. Killing by taking away oxygen
PRESUMPTUOUS	20. Going beyond what is right or proper; excessively forward

Light in the Forest Vocabulary Fill In The Blank 3

1. Hang about; wait nearby
2. Acting with secrecy to avoid notice
3. Temperament; usual mood
4. Brooding; morose; sulky
5. To want something that belongs to another
6. A feeling of extreme repugnance accompanied by avoidance
7. Tied up
8. Boldly resisting
9. To overlook, forgive, or disregard without protest
10. Stained; infected; spoiled
11. Pleading in protest
12. The place to which one is going
13. A twisting of the face that expresses pain, contempt, or disgust
14. Purifying; cleansing
15. Effort
16. Distant physically or emotionally; reserved and remote
17. Deserving reward or praise
18. Recognized or comprehended mentally
19. Lowering the pride, dignity, or self-respect
20. Going beyond what is right or proper; excessively forward

Light in the Forest Vocabulary Fill In The Blank 3 Answer Key

HOVER	1. Hang about; wait nearby
STEALTHY	2. Acting with secrecy to avoid notice
DISPOSITION	3. Temperament; usual mood
SULLEN	4. Brooding; morose; sulky
COVET	5. To want something that belongs to another
AVERSION	6. A feeling of extreme repugnance accompanied by avoidance
TRUSSED	7. Tied up
DEFIANT	8. Boldly resisting
CONDONE	9. To overlook, forgive, or disregard without protest
TAINTED	10. Stained; infected; spoiled
REMONSTRATING	11. Pleading in protest
DESTINATION	12. The place to which one is going
GRIMACE	13. A twisting of the face that expresses pain, contempt, or disgust
PURGING	14. Purifying; cleansing
EXERTION	15. Effort
ALOOFNESS	16. Distant physically or emotionally; reserved and remote
MERITORIOUS	17. Deserving reward or praise
DISCERNED	18. Recognized or comprehended mentally
HUMILIATING	19. Lowering the pride, dignity, or self-respect
PRESUMPTUOUS	20. Going beyond what is right or proper; excessively forward

Light in the Forest Vocabulary Fill In The Blank 4

_____ 1. Threatening

_____ 2. Having supreme authority

_____ 3. Having an abnormally pale complexion

_____ 4. Relieving the sorrow or grief

_____ 5. A feeling of extreme repugnance accompanied by avoidance

_____ 6. Barren; lifeless

_____ 7. Not paying attention

_____ 8. Worthy of being imitated

_____ 9. Arousing strong dislike or intense displeasure

_____ 10. Hang about; wait nearby

_____ 11. Brooding; morose; sulky

_____ 12. Great afflictions or suffering

_____ 13. Distant physically or emotionally; reserved and remote

_____ 14. Distributed

_____ 15. To disturb, interfere with, or annoy

_____ 16. Payment

_____ 17. Twisted; misshapen

_____ 18. Act of bringing under control; conquering

_____ 19. Stained; infected; spoiled

_____ 20. A young tree

Light in the Forest Vocabulary Fill In The Blank 4 Answer Key

OMINOUS	1. Threatening
IMPERIAL	2. Having supreme authority
PALLID	3. Having an abnormally pale complexion
CONSOLATION	4. Relieving the sorrow or grief
AVERSION	5. A feeling of extreme repugnance accompanied by avoidance
DESOLATE	6. Barren; lifeless
HEEDLESS	7. Not paying attention
EXEMPLARY	8. Worthy of being imitated
ODIOUS	9. Arousing strong dislike or intense displeasure
HOVER	10. Hang about; wait nearby
SULLEN	11. Brooding; morose; sulky
TRIBULATIONS	12. Great afflictions or suffering
ALOOFNESS	13. Distant physically or emotionally; reserved and remote
ALLOTTED	14. Distributed
MOLEST	15. To disturb, interfere with, or annoy
REMUNERATION	16. Payment
DISTORTED	17. Twisted; misshapen
SUBJUGATION	18. Act of bringing under control; conquering
TAINTED	19. Stained; infected; spoiled
SAPLING	20. A young tree

Light in the Forest Vocabulary Matching 1

___ 1. MOLEST A. Dark; gloomy
___ 2. EXERTION B. Barren; lifeless
___ 3. DOUGHTIER C. Courage; bravery
___ 4. MERIDIAN D. Not paying attention
___ 5. DESOLATE E. To suffer patiently without yielding
___ 6. INSIDIOUS F. More courageous
___ 7. GRIMACE G. Advice
___ 8. INCREDULITY H. Worthy of being imitated
___ 9. COUNSEL I. Threatening
___ 10. VALOR J. Tied up
___ 11. MIASMAS K. Gloomily; without cheer
___ 12. BLEAKLY L. Highest point; peak
___ 13. HOVER M. One that is considered undesirable, obnoxious, or troublesome
___ 14. OMINOUS N. To disturb, interfere with, or annoy
___ 15. SOMBER O. Net for catching fish
___ 16. HEEDLESS P. Comfort in trouble
___ 17. SUBJUGATION Q. Hang about; wait nearby
___ 18. EXEMPLARY R. Intended to entrap; treacherous
___ 19. VARMINT S. A twisting of the face that expresses pain, contempt, or disgust
___ 20. TRIBULATIONS T. To want something that belongs to another
___ 21. SOLACE U. Effort
___ 22. COVET V. Disbelief
___ 23. ENDURE W. Act of bringing under control; conquering
___ 24. TRUSSED X. Great afflictions or suffering
___ 25. SEINE Y. Swamp gas; odor of decaying matter

Light in the Forest Vocabulary Matching 1 Answer Key

N - 1.	MOLEST	A. Dark; gloomy
U - 2.	EXERTION	B. Barren; lifeless
F - 3.	DOUGHTIER	C. Courage; bravery
L - 4.	MERIDIAN	D. Not paying attention
B - 5.	DESOLATE	E. To suffer patiently without yielding
R - 6.	INSIDIOUS	F. More courageous
S - 7.	GRIMACE	G. Advice
V - 8.	INCREDULITY	H. Worthy of being imitated
G - 9.	COUNSEL	I. Threatening
C - 10.	VALOR	J. Tied up
Y - 11.	MIASMAS	K. Gloomily; without cheer
K - 12.	BLEAKLY	L. Highest point; peak
Q - 13.	HOVER	M. One that is considered undesirable, obnoxious, or troublesome
I - 14.	OMINOUS	N. To disturb, interfere with, or annoy
A - 15.	SOMBER	O. Net for catching fish
D - 16.	HEEDLESS	P. Comfort in trouble
W - 17.	SUBJUGATION	Q. Hang about; wait nearby
H - 18.	EXEMPLARY	R. Intended to entrap; treacherous
M - 19.	VARMINT	S. A twisting of the face that expresses pain, contempt, or disgust
X - 20.	TRIBULATIONS	T. To want something that belongs to another
P - 21.	SOLACE	U. Effort
T - 22.	COVET	V. Disbelief
E - 23.	ENDURE	W. Act of bringing under control; conquering
J - 24.	TRUSSED	X. Great afflictions or suffering
O - 25.	SEINE	Y. Swamp gas; odor of decaying matter

Light in the Forest Vocabulary Matching 2

___ 1. MIASMAS   A. Having an abnormally pale complexion
___ 2. HEEDLESS   B. One that is considered undesirable, obnoxious, or troublesome
___ 3. DISCERNED   C. Lowering the pride, dignity, or self-respect
___ 4. IMPERIAL   D. To want something that belongs to another
___ 5. EXULTATION   E. Intended to entrap; treacherous
___ 6. FORMIDABLE   F. Net for catching fish
___ 7. ALOOFNESS   G. Having or revealing little emotion
___ 8. MOLEST   H. To disturb, interfere with, or annoy
___ 9. ABDUCTOR   I. Agreed
___10. STOLID   J. A conscious choice or decision
___11. VARMINT   K. Highest point; peak
___12. SEINE   L. Having supreme authority
___13. ODIOUS   M. Excited and often noisy activity
___14. COVET   N. Speed or quickness
___15. VOLITION   O. Deserving reward or praise
___16. MERIDIAN   P. Arousing fear, dread, or alarm
___17. HUMILIATING   Q. Distant physically or emotionally; reserved and remote
___18. BUSTLE   R. Arousing strong dislike or intense displeasure
___19. EXERTION   S. Kidnapper
___20. ASSENTED   T. Effort
___21. DESOLATE   U. Swamp gas; odor of decaying matter
___22. PALLID   V. Recognized or comprehended mentally
___23. INSIDIOUS   W. Rejoicing
___24. ALACRITY   X. Not paying attention
___25. MERITORIOUS   Y. Barren; lifeless

Light in the Forest Vocabulary Matching 2 Answer Key

U - 1.	MIASMAS	A. Having an abnormally pale complexion
X - 2.	HEEDLESS	B. One that is considered undesirable, obnoxious, or troublesome
V - 3.	DISCERNED	C. Lowering the pride, dignity, or self-respect
L - 4.	IMPERIAL	D. To want something that belongs to another
W - 5.	EXULTATION	E. Intended to entrap; treacherous
P - 6.	FORMIDABLE	F. Net for catching fish
Q - 7.	ALOOFNESS	G. Having or revealing little emotion
H - 8.	MOLEST	H. To disturb, interfere with, or annoy
S - 9.	ABDUCTOR	I. Agreed
G - 10.	STOLID	J. A conscious choice or decision
B - 11.	VARMINT	K. Highest point; peak
F - 12.	SEINE	L. Having supreme authority
R - 13.	ODIOUS	M. Excited and often noisy activity
D - 14.	COVET	N. Speed or quickness
J - 15.	VOLITION	O. Deserving reward or praise
K - 16.	MERIDIAN	P. Arousing fear, dread, or alarm
C - 17.	HUMILIATING	Q. Distant physically or emotionally; reserved and remote
M - 18.	BUSTLE	R. Arousing strong dislike or intense displeasure
T - 19.	EXERTION	S. Kidnapper
I - 20.	ASSENTED	T. Effort
Y - 21.	DESOLATE	U. Swamp gas; odor of decaying matter
A - 22.	PALLID	V. Recognized or comprehended mentally
E - 23.	INSIDIOUS	W. Rejoicing
N - 24.	ALACRITY	X. Not paying attention
O - 25.	MERITORIOUS	Y. Barren; lifeless

Light in the Forest Vocabulary Matching 3

___ 1. SUBJUGATION   A. Rejoicing
___ 2. PUNGENCY   B. Worthy of being imitated
___ 3. FILIAL   C. Twisted; misshapen
___ 4. EXEMPLARY   D. To disturb, interfere with, or annoy
___ 5. STOLID   E. Courage; bravery
___ 6. VALOR   F. Recognized or comprehended mentally
___ 7. EXERTION   G. Agreed
___ 8. MIASMAS   H. Pertaining to a son or daughter
___ 9. DEBASED   I. Prevented or discouraged from acting
___10. MOLEST   J. Arousing fear, dread, or alarm
___11. FORMIDABLE   K. Barren; lifeless
___12. EXULTATION   L. Evil
___13. GRIMACE   M. Stinging; capable of burning
___14. ALACRITY   N. Speed or quickness
___15. DETERRED   O. Act of bringing under control; conquering
___16. DESOLATE   P. Killing by taking away oxygen
___17. OMINOUS   Q. Lowered in character, quality, or value; degraded
___18. DISCERNED   R. Effort
___19. DISTORTED   S. Dark; gloomy
___20. SOMBER   T. A twisting of the face that expresses pain, contempt, or disgust
___21. SINISTER   U. Swamp gas; odor of decaying matter
___22. ASSENTED   V. Threatening
___23. SUFFOCATING   W. Kidnapper
___24. INSIDIOUS   X. Having or revealing little emotion
___25. ABDUCTOR   Y. Intended to entrap; treacherous

Light in the Forest Vocabulary Matching 3 Answer Key

O - 1.	SUBJUGATION	A. Rejoicing
M - 2.	PUNGENCY	B. Worthy of being imitated
H - 3.	FILIAL	C. Twisted; misshapen
B - 4.	EXEMPLARY	D. To disturb, interfere with, or annoy
X - 5.	STOLID	E. Courage; bravery
E - 6.	VALOR	F. Recognized or comprehended mentally
R - 7.	EXERTION	G. Agreed
U - 8.	MIASMAS	H. Pertaining to a son or daughter
Q - 9.	DEBASED	I. Prevented or discouraged from acting
D - 10.	MOLEST	J. Arousing fear, dread, or alarm
J - 11.	FORMIDABLE	K. Barren; lifeless
A - 12.	EXULTATION	L. Evil
T - 13.	GRIMACE	M. Stinging; capable of burning
N - 14.	ALACRITY	N. Speed or quickness
I - 15.	DETERRED	O. Act of bringing under control; conquering
K - 16.	DESOLATE	P. Killing by taking away oxygen
V - 17.	OMINOUS	Q. Lowered in character, quality, or value; degraded
F - 18.	DISCERNED	R. Effort
C - 19.	DISTORTED	S. Dark; gloomy
S - 20.	SOMBER	T. A twisting of the face that expresses pain, contempt, or disgust
L - 21.	SINISTER	U. Swamp gas; odor of decaying matter
G - 22.	ASSENTED	V. Threatening
P - 23.	SUFFOCATING	W. Kidnapper
Y - 24.	INSIDIOUS	X. Having or revealing little emotion
W - 25.	ABDUCTOR	Y. Intended to entrap; treacherous

Light in the Forest Vocabulary Matching 4

___ 1. TRUSSED A. Kidnapper
___ 2. VARMINT B. Arousing strong dislike or intense displeasure
___ 3. STEALTHY C. Tied up
___ 4. ALACRITY D. Burdens or obstacles
___ 5. ASSENTED E. Net for catching fish
___ 6. GRIMACE F. Worthy of being imitated
___ 7. ENCUMBRANCES G. Distributed
___ 8. DISCERNED H. Acting with secrecy to avoid notice
___ 9. IMPERIAL I. Speed or quickness
___10. FILIAL J. Pertaining to a son or daughter
___11. BUSTLE K. Recognized or comprehended mentally
___12. PUNGENCY L. Boastful display meant to impress others; showiness
___13. ODIOUS M. A twisting of the face that expresses pain, contempt, or disgust
___14. OMINOUS N. Great afflictions or suffering
___15. DISTORTED O. A young tree
___16. ENDURE P. Twisted; misshapen
___17. TRIBULATIONS Q. Threatening
___18. EXEMPLARY R. Having supreme authority
___19. SEINE S. Stinging; capable of burning
___20. SAPLING T. Excited and often noisy activity
___21. ALLOTTED U. Agreed
___22. SOLACE V. One that is considered undesirable, obnoxious, or troublesome
___23. ABDUCTOR W. Comfort in trouble
___24. REMONSTRATING X. Pleading in protest
___25. OSTENTATION Y. To suffer patiently without yielding

Light in the Forest Vocabulary Matching 4 Answer Key

C - 1.	TRUSSED	A. Kidnapper
V - 2.	VARMINT	B. Arousing strong dislike or intense displeasure
H - 3.	STEALTHY	C. Tied up
I - 4.	ALACRITY	D. Burdens or obstacles
U - 5.	ASSENTED	E. Net for catching fish
M - 6.	GRIMACE	F. Worthy of being imitated
D - 7.	ENCUMBRANCES	G. Distributed
K - 8.	DISCERNED	H. Acting with secrecy to avoid notice
R - 9.	IMPERIAL	I. Speed or quickness
J - 10.	FILIAL	J. Pertaining to a son or daughter
T - 11.	BUSTLE	K. Recognized or comprehended mentally
S - 12.	PUNGENCY	L. Boastful display meant to impress others; showiness
B - 13.	ODIOUS	M. A twisting of the face that expresses pain, contempt, or disgust
Q - 14.	OMINOUS	N. Great afflictions or suffering
P - 15.	DISTORTED	O. A young tree
Y - 16.	ENDURE	P. Twisted; misshapen
N - 17.	TRIBULATIONS	Q. Threatening
F - 18.	EXEMPLARY	R. Having supreme authority
E - 19.	SEINE	S. Stinging; capable of burning
O - 20.	SAPLING	T. Excited and often noisy activity
G - 21.	ALLOTTED	U. Agreed
W - 22.	SOLACE	V. One that is considered undesirable, obnoxious, or troublesome
A - 23.	ABDUCTOR	W. Comfort in trouble
X - 24.	REMONSTRATING	X. Pleading in protest
L - 25.	OSTENTATION	Y. To suffer patiently without yielding

Light in the Forest Vocabulary Magic Squares 1

A. VOLITION
B. DERISION
C. SUBJUGATION
D. SAPLING
E. IMPERIAL
F. GRIMACE
G. SULLEN
H. ABHORRENCE
I. LOATHING
J. FATHOM
K. DOUGHTIER
L. LACKEYS
M. COVET
N. ENDURE
O. TRUSSED
P. TRIBULATIONS

1. Ridicule
2. Brooding; morose; sulky
3. More courageous
4. To suffer patiently without yielding
5. To want something that belongs to another
6. Slaves; forced laborers
7. A feeling of repugnance or loathing
8. A conscious choice or decision
9. Great afflictions or suffering
10. Great dislike; abhorrence
11. Having supreme authority
12. A young tree
13. Act of bringing under control; conquering
14. A twisting of the face that expresses pain, contempt, or disgust
15. Understand
16. Tied up

A=	B=	C=	D=
E=	F=	G=	H=
I=	J=	K=	L=
M=	N=	O=	P=

Light in the Forest Vocabulary Magic Squares 1 Answer Key

A. VOLITION
B. DERISION
C. SUBJUGATION
D. SAPLING
E. IMPERIAL
F. GRIMACE
G. SULLEN
H. ABHORRENCE
I. LOATHING
J. FATHOM
K. DOUGHTIER
L. LACKEYS
M. COVET
N. ENDURE
O. TRUSSED
P. TRIBULATIONS

1. Ridicule
2. Brooding; morose; sulky
3. More courageous
4. To suffer patiently without yielding
5. To want something that belongs to another
6. Slaves; forced laborers
7. A feeling of repugnance or loathing
8. A conscious choice or decision
9. Great afflictions or suffering
10. Great dislike; abhorrence
11. Having supreme authority
12. A young tree
13. Act of bringing under control; conquering
14. A twisting of the face that expresses pain, contempt, or disgust
15. Understand
16. Tied up

A=8	B=1	C=13	D=12
E=11	F=14	G=2	H=7
I=10	J=15	K=3	L=6
M=5	N=4	O=16	P=9

Light in the Forest Vocabulary Magic Squares 2

A. BLEAKLY
B. SUBJUGATION
C. PRECEPTS
D. ENCUMBRANCES
E. HOVER
F. FORMIDABLE
G. BERATING
H. OSTENTATION
I. FILIAL
J. VALOR
K. SOMBER
L. EXERTION
M. EXEMPLARY
N. COVET
O. VOLITION
P. HEEDLESS

1. Boastful display meant to impress others; showiness
2. Gloomily; without cheer
3. Act of bringing under control; conquering
4. Scolding; belittling
5. Courage; bravery
6. A conscious choice or decision
7. Not paying attention
8. Pertaining to a son or daughter
9. Dark; gloomy
10. To want something that belongs to another
11. Worthy of being imitated
12. Effort
13. Hang about; wait nearby
14. Burdens or obstacles
15. Rules or principles
16. Arousing fear, dread, or alarm

A=	B=	C=	D=
E=	F=	G=	H=
I=	J=	K=	L=
M=	N=	O=	P=

Light in the Forest Vocabulary Magic Squares 2 Answer Key

A. BLEAKLY
B. SUBJUGATION
C. PRECEPTS
D. ENCUMBRANCES
E. HOVER
F. FORMIDABLE
G. BERATING
H. OSTENTATION
I. FILIAL
J. VALOR
K. SOMBER
L. EXERTION
M. EXEMPLARY
N. COVET
O. VOLITION
P. HEEDLESS

1. Boastful display meant to impress others; showiness
2. Gloomily; without cheer
3. Act of bringing under control; conquering
4. Scolding; belittling
5. Courage; bravery
6. A conscious choice or decision
7. Not paying attention
8. Pertaining to a son or daughter
9. Dark; gloomy
10. To want something that belongs to another
11. Worthy of being imitated
12. Effort
13. Hang about; wait nearby
14. Burdens or obstacles
15. Rules or principles
16. Arousing fear, dread, or alarm

A=2	B=3	C=15	D=14
E=13	F=16	G=4	H=1
I=8	J=5	K=9	L=12
M=11	N=10	O=6	P=7

Light in the Forest Vocabulary Magic Squares 3

A. APPEASE
B. BLEAKLY
C. DETERRED
D. OMINOUS
E. PRESUMPTUOUS
F. DERISION
G. COVET
H. FORMIDABLE
I. VARMINT
J. ASSENTED
K. ABHORRENCE
L. GRIMACE
M. ENCUMBRANCES
N. CONDONE
O. STOLID
P. SEINE

1. Having or revealing little emotion
2. Threatening
3. Agreed
4. Going beyond what is right or proper; excessively forward
5. One that is considered undesirable, obnoxious, or troublesome
6. Ridicule
7. Net for catching fish
8. Prevented or discouraged from acting
9. Arousing fear, dread, or alarm
10. A feeling of repugnance or loathing
11. Pacify; soothe
12. To overlook, forgive, or disregard without protest
13. Gloomily; without cheer
14. Burdens or obstacles
15. To want something that belongs to another
16. A twisting of the face that expresses pain, contempt, or disgust

A=	B=	C=	D=
E=	F=	G=	H=
I=	J=	K=	L=
M=	N=	O=	P=

Light in the Forest Vocabulary Magic Suqares 3 Answer Key

A. APPEASE
B. BLEAKLY
C. DETERRED
D. OMINOUS
E. PRESUMPTUOUS
F. DERISION
G. COVET
H. FORMIDABLE
I. VARMINT
J. ASSENTED
K. ABHORRENCE
L. GRIMACE
M. ENCUMBRANCES
N. CONDONE
O. STOLID
P. SEINE

1. Having or revealing little emotion
2. Threatening
3. Agreed
4. Going beyond what is right or proper; excessively forward
5. One that is considered undesirable, obnoxious, or troublesome
6. Ridicule
7. Net for catching fish
8. Prevented or discouraged from acting
9. Arousing fear, dread, or alarm
10. A feeling of repugnance or loathing
11. Pacify; soothe
12. To overlook, forgive, or disregard without protest
13. Gloomily; without cheer
14. Burdens or obstacles
15. To want something that belongs to another
16. A twisting of the face that expresses pain, contempt, or disgust

A=11	B=13	C=8	D=2
E=4	F=6	G=15	H=9
I=5	J=3	K=10	L=16
M=14	N=12	O=1	P=7

Light in the Forest Vocabulary Magic Squares 4

A. SOLACE
B. PURGING
C. PRECEPTS
D. MERITORIOUS
E. PALLID
F. OSTENTATION
G. DOUGHTIER
H. SEINE
I. TRUSSED
J. CONDONE
K. MOLEST
L. VERMILION
M. EXEMPLARY
N. MIASMAS
O. PESTILENCE
P. SUBJUGATION

1. Comfort in trouble
2. Swamp gas; odor of decaying matter
3. To overlook, forgive, or disregard without protest
4. Having an abnormally pale complexion
5. More courageous
6. A vivid red to reddish orange
7. Act of bringing under control; conquering
8. Rules or principles
9. A destructive, evil influence
10. Deserving reward or praise
11. Net for catching fish
12. To disturb, interfere with, or annoy
13. Tied up
14. Boastful display meant to impress others; showiness
15. Purifying; cleansing
16. Worthy of being imitated

A=	B=	C=	D=
E=	F=	G=	H=
I=	J=	K=	L=
M=	N=	O=	P=

Light in the Forest Vocabulary Magic Squares 4 Answer Key

A. SOLACE
B. PURGING
C. PRECEPTS
D. MERITORIOUS
E. PALLID
F. OSTENTATION
G. DOUGHTIER
H. SEINE
I. TRUSSED
J. CONDONE
K. MOLEST
L. VERMILION
M. EXEMPLARY
N. MIASMAS
O. PESTILENCE
P. SUBJUGATION

1. Comfort in trouble
2. Swamp gas; odor of decaying matter
3. To overlook, forgive, or disregard without protest
4. Having an abnormally pale complexion
5. More courageous
6. A vivid red to reddish orange
7. Act of bringing under control; conquering
8. Rules or principles
9. A destructive, evil influence
10. Deserving reward or praise
11. Net for catching fish
12. To disturb, interfere with, or annoy
13. Tied up
14. Boastful display meant to impress others; showiness
15. Purifying; cleansing
16. Worthy of being imitated

A=1	B=15	C=8	D=10
E=4	F=14	G=5	H=11
I=13	J=3	K=12	L=6
M=16	N=2	O=9	P=7

Light in the Forest Vocabulary Word Search 1

```
Y L A C K E Y S T O L I D V A R M I N T
C K P O S C N E V G N I T A R E B T O S
S G P N H I V Z M Z A Y T N O B V V M Q
U W E S S O N E S V I P K D D M R L I M
L R A O C L X I O T D T E T I O K N N Q
L Z S L B E H L S N I N R P O S O V O C
E T E A R Q I E P T R Q C U U I S W U F
N O I T A T L U X E E E L T S U B Y S Z
L W I I I O R M C C M R R R B S L S U C
L O W O M G J S N A V E E J W E E L O T
N Y N N I A I E N L V V U P D L A D I C
M W V N F D L L Q O A G K R D B K F R G
O I G O T I E L H S A Y D E I A L I O F
H C A I T F G F O T N E E C S D Y L T T
T R R S V W G R I T S H O E T I P I I K
A V E I M V B O I A T U C P O M A A R W
F P D R X A N W B M N E J T R R L L E Q
N G L E W L S E X S A T D S T O L Q M X
K Z R D Y O D S E Z P C N G E F I V S H
K E N D U R E L S E I N E S D L D F K Y
```

A conscious choice or decision (8)
A destructive, evil influence (10)
A feeling of extreme repugnance accompanied by avoidance (8)
A twisting of the face that expresses pain, contempt, or disgust (7)
Act of bringing under control; conquering (11)
Advice (7)
Arousing fear, dread, or alarm (10)
Arousing strong dislike or intense displeasure (6)
Boldly resisting (7)
Brooding; morose; sulky (6)
Comfort in trouble (6)
Courage; bravery (5)
Dark; gloomy (6)
Deserving reward or praise (11)
Distributed (8)
Effort (8)
Evil (8)
Excited and often noisy activity (6)
Gloomily; without cheer (7)
Hang about; wait nearby (5)
Having an abnormally pale complexion (6)
Having or revealing little emotion (6)
Highest point; peak (8)

Lowered in character, quality, or value; degraded (7)
Net for catching fish (5)
Not paying attention (8)
One that is considered undesirable, obnoxious, or troublesome (7)
Pacify; soothe (7)
Pertaining to a son or daughter (6)
Purifying; cleansing (7)
Recognized or comprehended mentally (9)
Rejoicing (10)
Relieving the sorrow or grief (11)
Ridicule (8)
Rules or principles (8)
Scolding; belittling (8)
Slaves; forced laborers (7)
Swamp gas; odor of decaying matter (7)
Threatening (7)
Tied up (7)
To disturb, interfere with, or annoy (6)
To suffer patiently without yielding (6)
To want something that belongs to another (5)
Twisted; misshapen (9)
Understand (6)

Light in the Forest Vocabulary Word Search 1 Answer Key

A conscious choice or decision (8)
A destructive, evil influence (10)
A feeling of extreme repugnance accompanied by avoidance (8)
A twisting of the face that expresses pain, contempt, or disgust (7)
Act of bringing under control; conquering (11)
Advice (7)
Arousing fear, dread, or alarm (10)
Arousing strong dislike or intense displeasure (6)
Boldly resisting (7)
Brooding; morose; sulky (6)
Comfort in trouble (6)
Courage; bravery (5)
Dark; gloomy (6)
Deserving reward or praise (11)
Distributed (8)
Effort (8)
Evil (8)
Excited and often noisy activity (6)
Gloomily; without cheer (7)
Hang about; wait nearby (5)
Having an abnormally pale complexion (6)
Having or revealing little emotion (6)
Highest point; peak (8)

Lowered in character, quality, or value; degraded (7)
Net for catching fish (5)
Not paying attention (8)
One that is considered undesirable, obnoxious, or troublesome (7)
Pacify; soothe (7)
Pertaining to a son or daughter (6)
Purifying; cleansing (7)
Recognized or comprehended mentally (9)
Rejoicing (10)
Relieving the sorrow or grief (11)
Ridicule (8)
Rules or principles (8)
Scolding; belittling (8)
Slaves; forced laborers (7)
Swamp gas; odor of decaying matter (7)
Threatening (7)
Tied up (7)
To disturb, interfere with, or annoy (6)
To suffer patiently without yielding (6)
To want something that belongs to another (5)
Twisted; misshapen (9)
Understand (6)

Light in the Forest Vocabulary Word Search 2

```
T W R D A L O O F N E S S S F W V M R Z
Q G E E C N G G R Q G S U O I D O O D Z
M K B S C L N M J N S W D E E H T F G Y
B Z M O O N I M I Y Y E N S T C I F S H
D U O L N L T T N P T D A A U L W Y O V
M Q S A S T A D S N U E F D I J E V K N
F B J T O I R I E R P B B A D K E D W K
E C N E L I T S E P S A L A C R I T Y C
S N F I A E S T A S S S L A K L V H C D
F G M V T A N O V P E E L L O T T E N T
S U O N I M O R E J L D G T I L B N E M
H M H T O H M T R S D I S R A D T O G G
D E M R N Y E E M U E L N E I E Z D N Q
E R V O Z X R D I O E E T G V M R N U K
S I Z A L C F H L I H S S O S D A O P Y
S D E N R E C S I D H N C O U E R C P G
U I Y G Q M S G O I Y U X X L O I C E Y
R A V Q N M I T N S R O J W L A L N D C
T N A I F E D N T N B C M A E W C M E M
R D E S T I N A T I O N V F N G S E K C
```

A destructive, evil influence (10)
A twisting of the face that expresses pain, contempt, or disgust (7)
A vivid red to reddish orange (9)
A young tree (7)
Acting with secrecy to avoid notice (8)
Advice (7)
Agreed (8)
Arousing strong dislike or intense displeasure (6)
Barren; lifeless (8)
Boldly resisting (7)
Brooding; morose; sulky (6)
Comfort in trouble (6)
Courage; bravery (5)
Dark; gloomy (6)
Distant physically or emotionally; reserved and remote (9)
Excited and often noisy activity (6)
Hang about; wait nearby (5)
Having an abnormally pale complexion (6)
Having or revealing little emotion (6)
Highest point; peak (8)
Intended to entrap; treacherous (9)
Kidnapper (8)
Lowered in character, quality, or value; degraded (7)
Lowering the pride, dignity, or self-respect (11)
Net for catching fish (5)
Not paying attention (8)
One that is considered undesirable, obnoxious, or troublesome (7)
Pacify; soothe (7)
Pertaining to a son or daughter (6)
Pleading in protest (13)
Recognized or comprehended mentally (9)
Relieving the sorrow or grief (11)
Slaves; forced laborers (7)
Speed or quickness (8)
Stinging; capable of burning (8)
The place to which one is going (11)
Threatening (7)
Tied up (7)
To disturb, interfere with, or annoy (6)
To overlook, forgive, or disregard without protest (7)
To suffer patiently without yielding (6)
To want something that belongs to another (5)
Twisted; misshapen (9)
Understand (6)

Light in the Forest Vocabulary Word Search 2 Answer Key

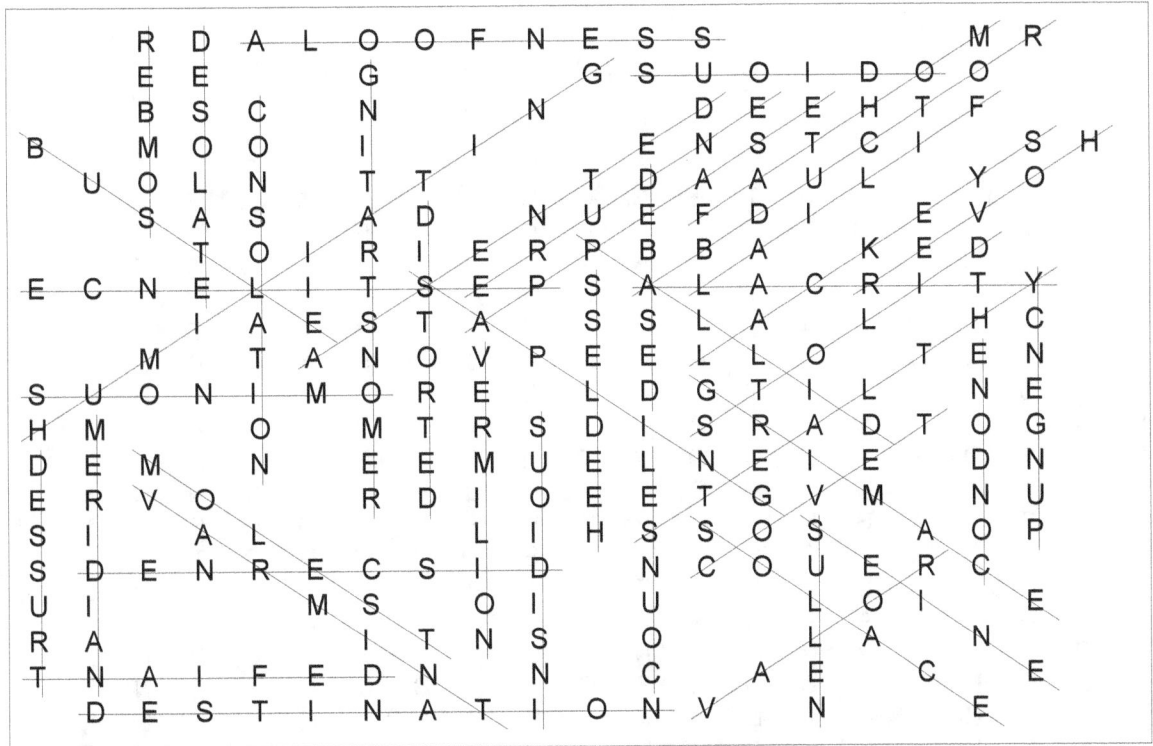

A destructive, evil influence (10)
A twisting of the face that expresses pain, contempt, or disgust (7)
A vivid red to reddish orange (9)
A young tree (7)
Acting with secrecy to avoid notice (8)
Advice (7)
Agreed (8)
Arousing strong dislike or intense displeasure (6)
Barren; lifeless (8)
Boldly resisting (7)
Brooding; morose; sulky (6)
Comfort in trouble (6)
Courage; bravery (5)
Dark; gloomy (6)
Distant physically or emotionally; reserved and remote (9)
Excited and often noisy activity (6)
Hang about; wait nearby (5)
Having an abnormally pale complexion (6)
Having or revealing little emotion (6)
Highest point; peak (8)
Intended to entrap; treacherous (9)
Kidnapper (8)
Lowered in character, quality, or value; degraded (7)
Lowering the pride, dignity, or self-respect (11)
Net for catching fish (5)
Not paying attention (8)
One that is considered undesirable, obnoxious, or troublesome (7)
Pacify; soothe (7)
Pertaining to a son or daughter (6)
Pleading in protest (13)
Recognized or comprehended mentally (9)
Relieving the sorrow or grief (11)
Slaves; forced laborers (7)
Speed or quickness (8)
Stinging; capable of burning (8)
The place to which one is going (11)
Threatening (7)
Tied up (7)
To disturb, interfere with, or annoy (6)
To overlook, forgive, or disregard without protest (7)
To suffer patiently without yielding (6)
To want something that belongs to another (5)
Twisted; misshapen (9)
Understand (6)

Light in the Forest Vocabulary Word Search 3

```
V E R M I L I O N D F H L V D F B H L L
V B E R A T I N G Z C O Q A S R V Y A Q
X J D R S T I S G B F L R M E U I C C Y
E N I D S T D M G S L E I M D H L N V Q
X P L E S S V E A M S G U I I I O L C W
E O O F S J T H T E S G N I N F D R V E C
M M T I J P I P E N E L S T B X A Y E N
P S S A P M J P N I R A T D T U G B Z R
L N U N T K A T T A P R B A E E O S G L P
A O O T K M E A T T T N E H V B A M T N E
R I I K X D C I V B G I F D O E A L B L F
Y T D X O O G T N T E O V C R R S T E E
R A O F N Y X I R N B T N Y C R E I D R Y
E L F D X A H D O U G H T I E Y D X N O H
T U S E I T L D E N S I Q A Y D X E C N
S B S S A S N O I R L S F L I Q E N T C E
I I E O A O C L O U I S E Q M N R T E L
N R L L C P E D F U S R D N B T P C R E V
I T D A J A A E R O N N S I O T L I E U L V
S S E T S V R C O N Y E I O E E O C D P
Y O E E L C D D R E E T S S N A N E N H
F L H H N H I L K I I D N S Y K W R E N B
J A X I V S N C Q L T U Z D S L T P Y B N
V C J H N J A F O W O Y Z L T Y N G Y B N
D E Q I R L M V Y C N E G N U P F J B F
```

ABHORRENCE	DERISION	INCREDULITY	SOLACE
ALACRITY	DESOLATE	INSIDIOUS	SOMBER
ALOOFNESS	DESTINATION	LACKEYS	STEALTHY
APPEASE	DETERRED	LOATHING	STOLID
ASSENTED	DISCERNED	MIASMAS	SUFFOCATING
AVERSION	DOUGHTIER	MOLEST	SULLEN
BERATING	ENDURE	ODIOUS	TAINTED
BLEAKLY	EXEMPLARY	PALLID	TRIBULATIONS
BUSTLE	EXERTION	PRECEPTS	TRUSSED
CONDONE	FATHOM	PUNGENCY	VALOR
COUNSEL	FILIAL	REMUNERATION	VARMINT
COVET	FORMIDABLE	SAPLING	VERMILION
DEBASED	HEEDLESS	SEINE	VOLITION
DEFIANT	HOVER	SINISTER	

Light in the Forest Vocabulary Word Search 3 Answer Key

ABHORRENCE	DERISION	INCREDULITY	SOLACE
ALACRITY	DESOLATE	INSIDIOUS	SOMBER
ALOOFNESS	DESTINATION	LACKEYS	STEALTHY
APPEASE	DETERRED	LOATHING	STOLID
ASSENTED	DISCERNED	MIASMAS	SUFFOCATING
AVERSION	DOUGHTIER	MOLEST	SULLEN
BERATING	ENDURE	ODIOUS	TAINTED
BLEAKLY	EXEMPLARY	PALLID	TRIBULATIONS
BUSTLE	EXERTION	PRECEPTS	TRUSSED
CONDONE	FATHOM	PUNGENCY	VALOR
COUNSEL	FILIAL	REMUNERATION	VARMINT
COVET	FORMIDABLE	SAPLING	VERMILION
DEBASED	HEEDLESS	SEINE	VOLITION
DEFIANT	HOVER	SINISTER	

Light in the Forest Vocabulary Word Search 4

```
R E M U N E R A T I O N L O A T H I N G
B L E A K L Y L B F I L I A L T R Z O D
X X G W J T J L W D D G D S Z I F I X
W M R K T S B O P F U D M S S R S L J
P X I W B U S T H A B C E Z I C W I C
D H M B N B W T P B L N T R E M C M Y
E N A I D R E M B F L E O R D T V R X
T X C H Q W X D F O Z D I N R A P A E Y
E D E B A S E D O S J R E D I Q G R V C
R K C M S D H L M E L D I N D N E M O N
R B O C P X A O X I B T M I F N I S G
E K N X K L V V N L E C G P T D N T T
D S S D T N A I F E D N R K F E U T E Q
S R O X R L S R S R U E A E N R R N N
R E L G O A S N Y A P Y B V T Y E I T S
E T A R P S U L L E N C M V S I S X A S
I S T L B O O N C P X N O O A N N B T L
T I I E C C N T O P X E S L M S H G I B
H N O T M O I K V A V G R I S I O O N R
G I N A P N M G E F N N N T A D T S N L
U S L L V D O N T A M U S I I I C L Q
O F L O M O L E S T L P Y O M O S A B Z
D A S S E N T E D H Z V U N X U N C B J
S T P E C E R P F O K S N O I S R E V A
M G W D I L O T S M E R I T O R I O U S
```

ABDUCTOR
ALLOTTED
ALOOFNESS
APPEASE
ASSENTED
AVERSION
BERATING
BLEAKLY
BUSTLE
CONDONE
CONSOLATION
COUNSEL
COVET
DEBASED

DEFIANT
DERISION
DESOLATE
DETERRED
DISCERNED
DOUGHTIER
ENDURE
EXEMPLARY
EXERTION
FATHOM
FILIAL
GRIMACE
HOVER
IMPERIAL

INSIDIOUS
LACKEYS
LOATHING
MERIDIAN
MERITORIOUS
MIASMAS
MOLEST
ODIOUS
OMINOUS
OSTENTATION
PALLID
PRECEPTS
PUNGENCY
PURGING

REMUNERATION
SAPLING
SEINE
SINISTER
SOLACE
SOMBER
STOLID
SULLEN
TAINTED
TRUSSED
VALOR
VARMINT
VERMILION
VOLITION

Light in the Forest Vocabulary Word Search 4 Answer Key

ABDUCTOR	DEFIANT	INSIDIOUS	REMUNERATION
ALLOTTED	DERISION	LACKEYS	SAPLING
ALOOFNESS	DESOLATE	LOATHING	SEINE
APPEASE	DETERRED	MERIDIAN	SINISTER
ASSENTED	DISCERNED	MERITORIOUS	SOLACE
AVERSION	DOUGHTIER	MIASMAS	SOMBER
BERATING	ENDURE	MOLEST	STOLID
BLEAKLY	EXEMPLARY	ODIOUS	SULLEN
BUSTLE	EXERTION	OMINOUS	TAINTED
CONDONE	FATHOM	OSTENTATION	TRUSSED
CONSOLATION	FILIAL	PALLID	VALOR
COUNSEL	GRIMACE	PRECEPTS	VARMINT
COVET	HOVER	PUNGENCY	VERMILION
DEBASED	IMPERIAL	PURGING	VOLITION

Light in the Forest Vocabulary Crossword 1

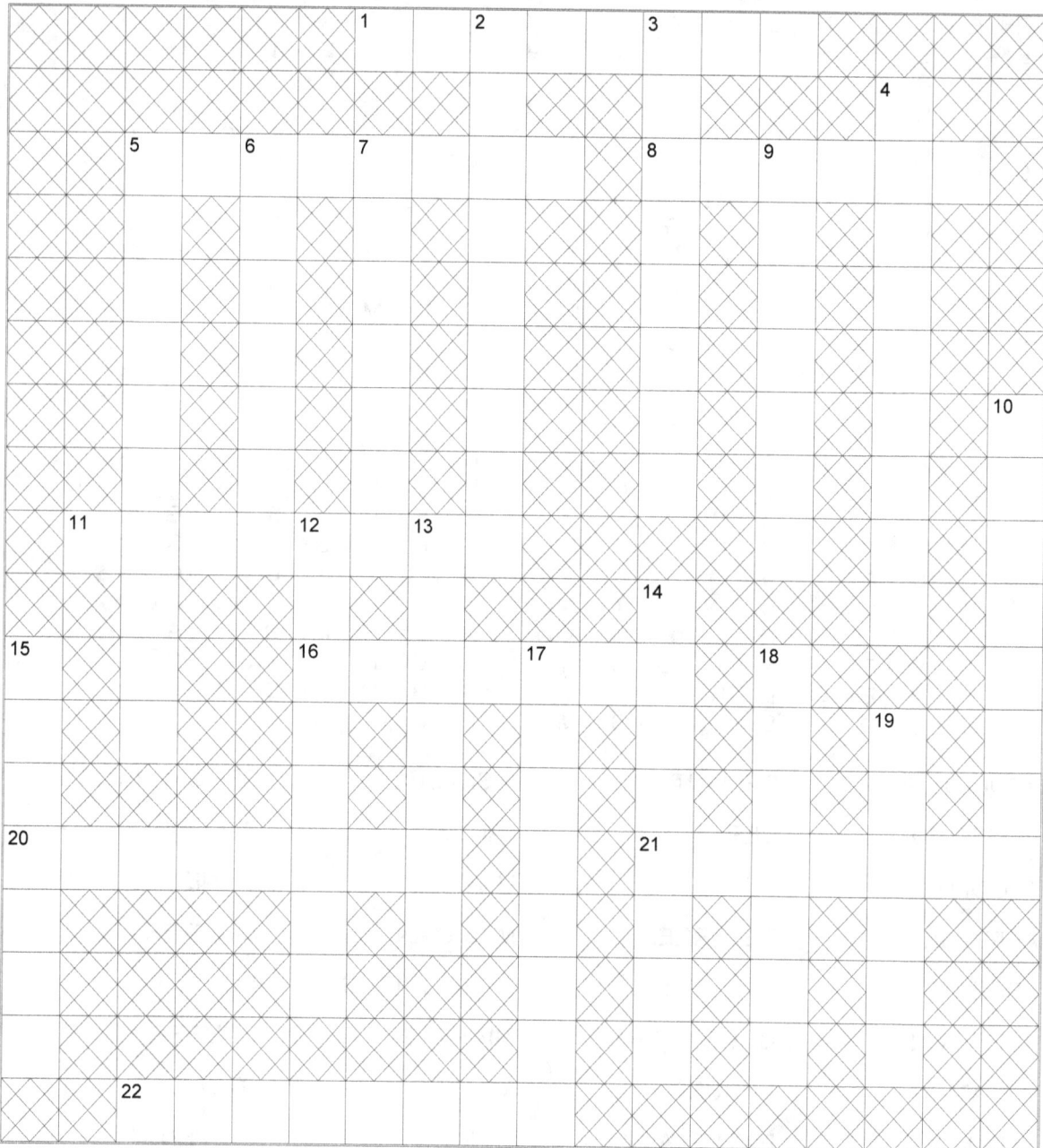

Across
1. Speed or quickness
5. Kidnapper
8. Having an abnormally pale complexion
11. Not paying attention
16. Pacify; soothe
20. A feeling of extreme repugnance accompanied by avoidance
21. Stained; infected; spoiled
22. Prevented or discouraged from acting

Down
2. Distant physically or emotionally; reserved and remote
3. Having supreme authority
4. Recognized or comprehended mentally
5. A feeling of repugnance or loathing
6. Lowered in character, quality, or value; degraded
7. To overlook, forgive, or disregard without protest
9. Slaves; forced laborers
10. Agreed
12. Great dislike; abhorrence
13. A young tree
14. Scolding; belittling
15. Gloomily; without cheer
17. Distributed
18. Boldly resisting
19. Understand

Light in the Forest Vocabulary Crossword 1 Answer Key

				1 A	2 L	A	C	3 R	I	T	Y		
					L			M			4 D		
	5 A		6 B		7 C	T	O	R	8 P	A	9 L	L	I	D
	A	B	D	U	C	T	O	R	P	A	L	L	I	D
	B		E		O				E		A		S	
	H		B		N		F		R		C		C	
	O		A		D		N		I		K		E	
	R		S		O		E		A		E		R	10 A
	R		E		N		S		L		Y		N	S
		11 H	E	E	D	12 L	E	13 S	S				S	S
			N			O		A		14 B			D	E
15 B		C			16 A	P	P	E	17 A	S	E	18 D		N
L		E			T			L		E		19 F		T
E					H			I		R		A		E
20 A	V	E	R	S	I	O	N		O		21 T	A	I	N	T	E	D
K					N		G		T		I		A		H		
L					G				T		N		N		O		
Y									E		G		T		M		
		22 D	E	T	E	R	R	E	D								

Across
1. Speed or quickness
5. Kidnapper
8. Having an abnormally pale complexion
11. Not paying attention
16. Pacify; soothe
20. A feeling of extreme repugnance accompanied by avoidance
21. Stained; infected; spoiled
22. Prevented or discouraged from acting

Down
2. Distant physically or emotionally; reserved and remote
3. Having supreme authority
4. Recognized or comprehended mentally
5. A feeling of repugnance or loathing
6. Lowered in character, quality, or value; degraded
7. To overlook, forgive, or disregard without protest
9. Slaves; forced laborers
10. Agreed
12. Great dislike; abhorrence
13. A young tree
14. Scolding; belittling
15. Gloomily; without cheer
17. Distributed
18. Boldly resisting
19. Understand

Light in the Forest Vocabulary Crossword 2

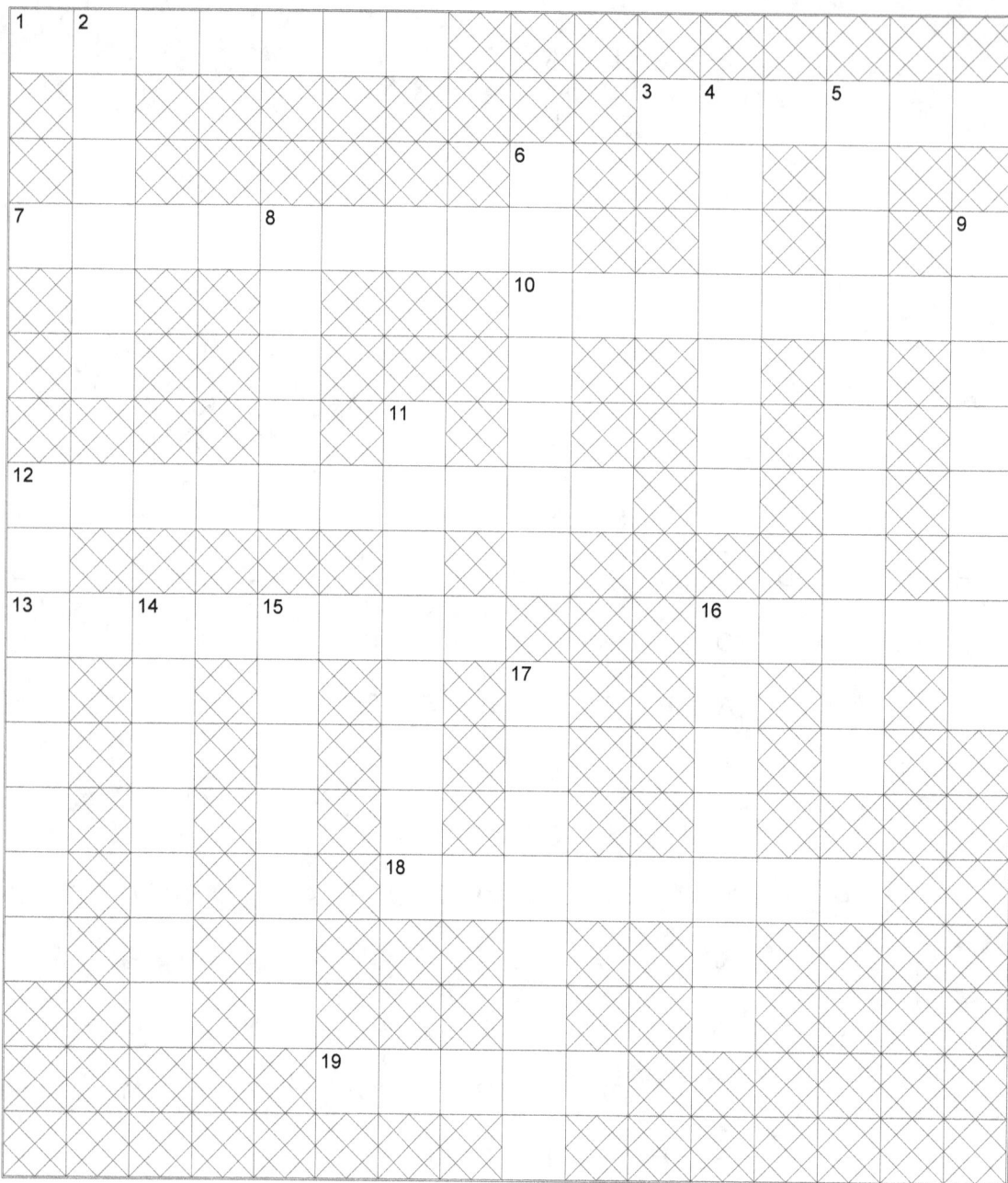

Across
1. To overlook, forgive, or disregard without protest
3. Understand
7. More courageous
10. Having supreme authority
12. A feeling of repugnance or loathing
13. Kidnapper
16. Net for catching fish
18. Effort
19. To want something that belongs to another

Down
2. Arousing strong dislike or intense displeasure
4. Pacify; soothe
5. Lowering the pride, dignity, or self-respect
6. A twisting of the face that expresses pain, contempt, or disgust
8. Hang about; wait nearby
9. Distributed
11. Barren; lifeless
12. Speed or quickness
14. Lowered in character, quality, or value; degraded
15. Advice
16. A young tree
17. Agreed

Light in the Forest Vocabulary Crossword 2 Answer Key

Across
1. To overlook, forgive, or disregard without protest
3. Understand
7. More courageous
10. Having supreme authority
12. A feeling of repugnance or loathing
13. Kidnapper
16. Net for catching fish
18. Effort
19. To want something that belongs to another

Down
2. Arousing strong dislike or intense displeasure
4. Pacify; soothe
5. Lowering the pride, dignity, or self-respect
6. A twisting of the face that expresses pain, contempt, or disgust
8. Hang about; wait nearby
9. Distributed
11. Barren; lifeless
12. Speed or quickness
14. Lowered in character, quality, or value; degraded
15. Advice
16. A young tree
17. Agreed

Light in the Forest Vocabulary Crossword 3

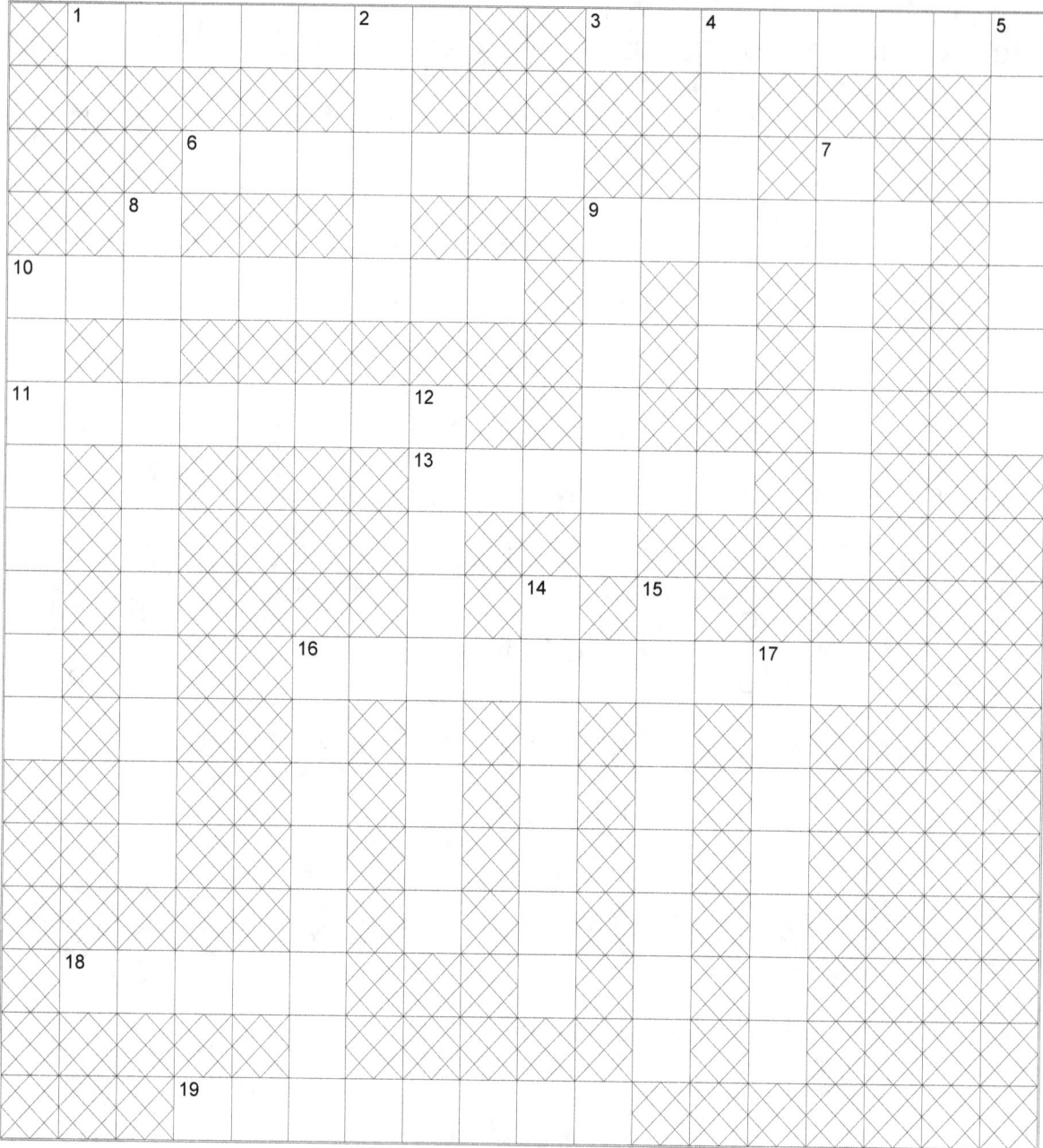

Across
1. Pacify; soothe
3. Having supreme authority
6. Boldly resisting
9. Pertaining to a son or daughter
10. Distant physically or emotionally; reserved and remote
11. Agreed
13. Arousing strong dislike or intense displeasure
16. A feeling of repugnance or loathing
18. To want something that belongs to another
19. Kidnapper

Down
2. Net for catching fish
4. Having an abnormally pale complexion
5. Slaves; forced laborers
7. A young tree
8. Relieving the sorrow or grief
9. Understand
10. Speed or quickness
12. More courageous
14. A twisting of the face that expresses pain, contempt, or disgust
15. Scolding; belittling
16. Distributed
17. To overlook, forgive, or disregard without protest

Light in the Forest Vocabulary Crossword 3 Answer Key

	1 A	P	P	E	2 A S E		3 I	M	4 P E	R	I	A	5 L
					E				A				A
		6 D	E	F	I	A	N	T		L		7 S		C
	8 C			N			9 F	I	L	I	A	L		K
10 A	L	O	O	F	N	E	S	S		A		I		P		E
L		N						T		D		L		Y
11 A	S	S	E	N	T	E	D	12 D		H				I		S
C		O				13 O	D	I	O	U	S		N		
R		L				U				M				G	
I		A				G		14 G		15 B				
T		T			16 A	B	H	O	R	R	E	N	17 C	E
Y		I			L		T			I			R		O
		O			L		I			M			A		N
		N			O		E			A			T		D
					T		R			C			I		O
	18 C	O	V	E	T					E			N		N
					E								G		E
			19 A	B	D	U	C	T	O	R			

Across
1. Pacify; soothe
3. Having supreme authority
6. Boldly resisting
9. Pertaining to a son or daughter
10. Distant physically or emotionally; reserved and remote
11. Agreed
13. Arousing strong dislike or intense displeasure
16. A feeling of repugnance or loathing
18. To want something that belongs to another
19. Kidnapper

Down
2. Net for catching fish
4. Having an abnormally pale complexion
5. Slaves; forced laborers
7. A young tree
8. Relieving the sorrow or grief
9. Understand
10. Speed or quickness
12. More courageous
14. A twisting of the face that expresses pain, contempt, or disgust
15. Scolding; belittling
16. Distributed
17. To overlook, forgive, or disregard without protest

Light in the Forest Vocabulary Crossword 4

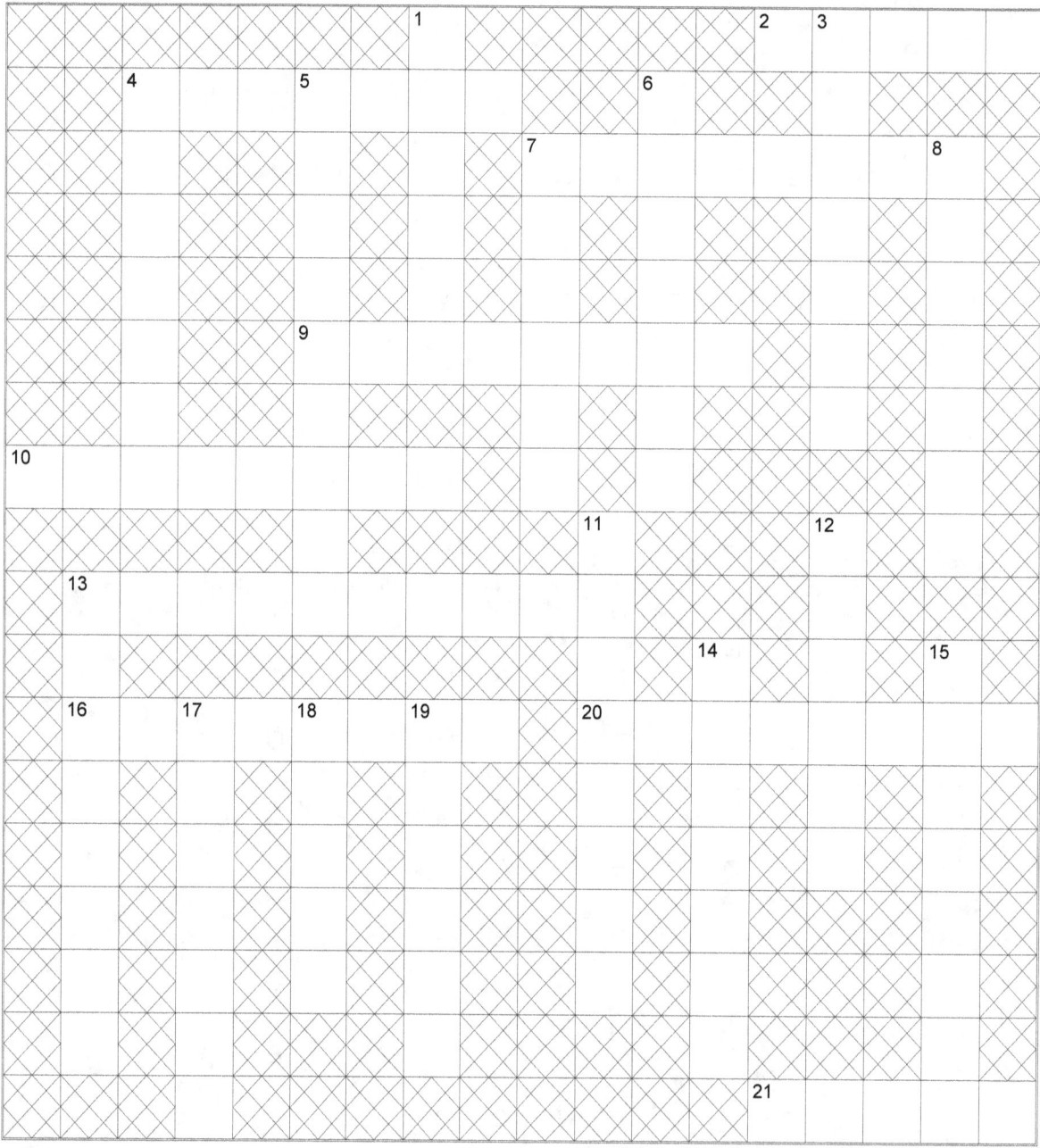

Across
2. Courage; bravery
4. To overlook, forgive, or disregard without protest
7. Rules or principles
9. Not paying attention
10. A conscious choice or decision
13. A feeling of repugnance or loathing
16. Kidnapper
20. Distributed
21. Net for catching fish

Down
1. To suffer patiently without yielding
3. Pacify; soothe
4. Advice
5. More courageous
6. Lowered in character, quality, or value; degraded
7. Having an abnormally pale complexion
8. A young tree
11. Scolding; belittling
12. Excited and often noisy activity
13. Speed or quickness
14. Gloomily; without cheer
15. Ridicule
17. Boldly resisting
18. To want something that belongs to another
19. Arousing strong dislike or intense displeasure

Light in the Forest Vocabulary Crossword 4 Answer Key

(Crossword grid with the following answers)

Across
- 2. VALOR
- 4. CONDONE
- 7. PRECEPTS
- 9. HEEDLESS
- 10. VOLITION
- 13. ABHORRENCE
- 16. ABDUCTOR
- 20. ALLOTTED
- 21. SEINE

Down
- 1. ENDURE
- 3. RELAX (?)
- 4. COUNSEL
- 5. DOUGHTIER
- 6. DEBASED
- 7. PALLID
- 8. SAPLING
- 11. BERATING
- 12. BUSTLE
- 13. ABHORRENCE (down: ALACRITY)
- 14. BLEAKLY
- 15. DERISION
- 17. DEFIANT
- 18. COVETOUS
- 19. ODIOUS

Across
- 2. Courage; bravery
- 4. To overlook, forgive, or disregard without protest
- 7. Rules or principles
- 9. Not paying attention
- 10. A conscious choice or decision
- 13. A feeling of repugnance or loathing
- 16. Kidnapper
- 20. Distributed
- 21. Net for catching fish

Down
- 1. To suffer patiently without yielding
- 3. Pacify; soothe
- 4. Advice
- 5. More courageous
- 6. Lowered in character, quality, or value; degraded
- 7. Having an abnormally pale complexion
- 8. A young tree
- 11. Scolding; belittling
- 12. Excited and often noisy activity
- 13. Speed or quickness
- 14. Gloomily; without cheer
- 15. Ridicule
- 17. Boldly resisting
- 18. To want something that belongs to another
- 19. Arousing strong dislike or intense displeasure

Light in the Forest Vocabulary Juggle Letters 1

1. AENTNRROIMTGS = 1. _____
   Pleading in protest

2. UTRMPSUESPUO = 2. _____
   Going beyond what is right or proper; excessively forward

3. RTINAMV = 3. _____
   One that is considered undesirable, obnoxious, or troublesome

4. AMPXYEERL = 4. _____
   Worthy of being imitated

5. EOCTV = 5. _____
   To want something that belongs to another

6. NGPIURG = 6. _____
   Purifying; cleansing

7. NTEAXTIOLU = 7. _____
   Rejoicing

8. DOUIOS = 8. _____
   Arousing strong dislike or intense displeasure

9. IRASVOEN = 9. _____
   A feeling of extreme repugnance accompanied by avoidance

10. ERDNOISI = 10. _____
    Ridicule

11. AKYBLEL = 11. _____
    Gloomily; without cheer

12. DTTEANI = 12. _____
    Stained; infected; spoiled

13. LSETDOAE = 13. _____
    Barren; lifeless

14. STIPENECEL = 14. _____
    A destructive, evil influence

15. NNYPCEUG = 15. _____
    Stinging; capable of burning

Light in the Forest Vocabulary Juggle Letters 1 Answer Key

1. AENTNRROIMTGS = 1. REMONSTRATING
   Pleading in protest

2. UTRMPSUESPUO = 2. PRESUMPTUOUS
   Going beyond what is right or proper; excessively forward

3. RTINAMV = 3. VARMINT
   One that is considered undesirable, obnoxious, or troublesome

4. AMPXYEERL = 4. EXEMPLARY
   Worthy of being imitated

5. EOCTV = 5. COVET
   To want something that belongs to another

6. NGPIURG = 6. PURGING
   Purifying; cleansing

7. NTEAXTIOLU = 7. EXULTATION
   Rejoicing

8. DOUIOS = 8. ODIOUS
   Arousing strong dislike or intense displeasure

9. IRASVOEN = 9. AVERSION
   A feeling of extreme repugnance accompanied by avoidance

10. ERDNOISI = 10. DERISION
    Ridicule

11. AKYBLEL = 11. BLEAKLY
    Gloomily; without cheer

12. DTTEANI = 12. TAINTED
    Stained; infected; spoiled

13. LSETDOAE = 13. DESOLATE
    Barren; lifeless

14. STIPENECEL = 14. PESTILENCE
    A destructive, evil influence

15. NNYPCEUG = 15. PUNGENCY
    Stinging; capable of burning

Light in the Forest Vocabulary Juggle Letters 2

1. ULCINYTDREI = 1. _____
   Disbelief

2. LORDBFMIEA = 2. _____
   Arousing fear, dread, or alarm

3. TETDODSRI = 3. _____
   Twisted; misshapen

4. TAYHLSTE = 4. _____
   Acting with secrecy to avoid notice

5. LTBESU = 5. _____
   Excited and often noisy activity

6. CRAYATLI = 6. _____
   Speed or quickness

7. IARMNDEI = 7. _____
   Highest point; peak

8. ATIBEGNR = 8. _____
   Scolding; belittling

9. GURPNGI = 9. _____
   Purifying; cleansing

10. IDOUOS =10. _____
    Arousing strong dislike or intense displeasure

11. ERIINTSS =11. _____
    Evil

12. ALDEEOTS =12. _____
    Barren; lifeless

13. RMNTAVI =13. _____
    One that is considered undesirable, obnoxious, or troublesome

14. SCEYKAL =14. _____
    Slaves; forced laborers

15. IASGLPN =15. _____
    A young tree

Light in the Forest Vocabulary Juggle Letters 2 Answer Key

1. ULCINYTDREI = 1. INCREDULITY
Disbelief

2. LORDBFMIEA = 2. FORMIDABLE
Arousing fear, dread, or alarm

3. TETDODSRI = 3. DISTORTED
Twisted; misshapen

4. TAYHLSTE = 4. STEALTHY
Acting with secrecy to avoid notice

5. LTBESU = 5. BUSTLE
Excited and often noisy activity

6. CRAYATLI = 6. ALACRITY
Speed or quickness

7. IARMNDEI = 7. MERIDIAN
Highest point; peak

8. ATIBEGNR = 8. BERATING
Scolding; belittling

9. GURPNGI = 9. PURGING
Purifying; cleansing

10. IDOUOS = 10. ODIOUS
Arousing strong dislike or intense displeasure

11. ERIINTSS = 11. SINISTER
Evil

12. ALDEEOTS = 12. DESOLATE
Barren; lifeless

13. RMNTAVI = 13. VARMINT
One that is considered undesirable, obnoxious, or troublesome

14. SCEYKAL = 14. LACKEYS
Slaves; forced laborers

15. IASGLPN = 15. SAPLING
A young tree

Light in the Forest Vocabulary Juggle Letters 3

1. OLVITONI = 1. _____
   A conscious choice or decision

2. DSEHEELS = 2. _____
   Not paying attention

3. SPLGAIN = 3. _____
   A young tree

4. EEATDOSL = 4. _____
   Barren; lifeless

5. CAYSEKL = 5. _____
   Slaves; forced laborers

6. DRUYLICNIET = 6. _____
   Disbelief

7. LIEIRNOMV = 7. _____
   A vivid red to reddish orange

8. EOSCAL = 8. _____
   Comfort in trouble

9. THAMOF = 9. _____
   Understand

10. NBTGIARE =10. _____
    Scolding; belittling

11. NDATITE =11. _____
    Stained; infected; spoiled

12. OVLRA =12. _____
    Courage; bravery

13. NIADIMER =13. _____
    Highest point; peak

14. SNUECOL =14. _____
    Advice

15. ONINDITATES =15. _____
    The place to which one is going

Light in the Forest Vocabulary Juggle Letters 3 Answer Key

1. OLVITONI = 1. VOLITION
A conscious choice or decision

2. DSEHEELS = 2. HEEDLESS
Not paying attention

3. SPLGAIN = 3. SAPLING
A young tree

4. EEATDOSL = 4. DESOLATE
Barren; lifeless

5. CAYSEKL = 5. LACKEYS
Slaves; forced laborers

6. DRUYLICNIET = 6. INCREDULITY
Disbelief

7. LIEIRNOMV = 7. VERMILION
A vivid red to reddish orange

8. EOSCAL = 8. SOLACE
Comfort in trouble

9. THAMOF = 9. FATHOM
Understand

10. NBTGIARE = 10. BERATING
Scolding; belittling

11. NDATITE = 11. TAINTED
Stained; infected; spoiled

12. OVLRA = 12. VALOR
Courage; bravery

13. NIADIMER = 13. MERIDIAN
Highest point; peak

14. SNUECOL = 14. COUNSEL
Advice

15. ONINDITATES = 15. DESTINATION
The place to which one is going

Light in the Forest Vocabulary Juggle Letters 4

1. RHOEV = 1. _____
   Hang about; wait nearby

2. ENSEI = 2. _____
   Net for catching fish

3. ONODCEN = 3. _____
   To overlook, forgive, or disregard without protest

4. OCDTBUAR = 4. _____
   Kidnapper

5. NOOANLTCSIO = 5. _____
   Relieving the sorrow or grief

6. GYNNUCEP = 6. _____
   Stinging; capable of burning

7. GGINURP = 7. _____
   Purifying; cleansing

8. IOAENSVR = 8. _____
   A feeling of extreme repugnance accompanied by avoidance

9. DRTEUSS = 9. _____
   Tied up

10. NTAEDIF =10. _____
    Boldly resisting

11. ESNLEETICP =11. _____
    A destructive, evil influence

12. LIINOVOT =12. _____
    A conscious choice or decision

13. STINNAGRETMOR =13. _____
    Pleading in protest

14. IMAELRPI =14. _____
    Having supreme authority

15. OUSOID =15. _____
    Arousing strong dislike or intense displeasure

Light in the Forest Vocabulary Juggle Letters 4 Answer Key

1. RHOEV = 1. HOVER
Hang about; wait nearby

2. ENSEI = 2. SEINE
Net for catching fish

3. ONODCEN = 3. CONDONE
To overlook, forgive, or disregard without protest

4. OCDTBUAR = 4. ABDUCTOR
Kidnapper

5. NOOANLTCSIO = 5. CONSOLATION
Relieving the sorrow or grief

6. GYNNUCEP = 6. PUNGENCY
Stinging; capable of burning

7. GGINURP = 7. PURGING
Purifying; cleansing

8. IOAENSVR = 8. AVERSION
A feeling of extreme repugnance accompanied by avoidance

9. DRTEUSS = 9. TRUSSED
Tied up

10. NTAEDIF = 10. DEFIANT
Boldly resisting

11. ESNLEETICP = 11. PESTILENCE
A destructive, evil influence

12. LIINOVOT = 12. VOLITION
A conscious choice or decision

13. STINNAGRETMOR = 13. REMONSTRATING
Pleading in protest

14. IMAELRPI = 14. IMPERIAL
Having supreme authority

15. OUSOID = 15. ODIOUS
Arousing strong dislike or intense displeasure

ABDUCTOR	Kidnapper
ABHORRENCE	A feeling of repugnance or loathing
ALACRITY	Speed or quickness
ALLOTTED	Distributed
ALOOFNESS	Distant physically or emotionally; reserved and remote
APPEASE	Pacify; soothe

ASSENTED	Agreed
AVERSION	A feeling of extreme repugnance accompanied by avoidance
BERATING	Scolding; belittling
BLEAKLY	Gloomily; without cheer
BUSTLE	Excited and often noisy activity
CONDONE	To overlook, forgive, or disregard without protest

CONSOLATION	Relieving the sorrow or grief
COUNSEL	Advice
COVET	To want something that belongs to another
DEBASED	Lowered in character, quality, or value; degraded
DEFIANT	Boldly resisting
DERISION	Ridicule

DESOLATE	Barren; lifeless
DESTINATION	The place to which one is going
DETERRED	Prevented or discouraged from acting
DISCERNED	Recognized or comprehended mentally
DISPOSITION	Temperament; usual mood
DISTORTED	Twisted; misshapen

DOUGHTIER	More courageous
ENCUMBRANCES	Burdens or obstacles
ENDURE	To suffer patiently without yielding
EXEMPLARY	Worthy of being imitated
EXERTION	Effort
EXULTATION	Rejoicing

FATHOM	Understand
FILIAL	Pertaining to a son or daughter
FORMIDABLE	Arousing fear, dread, or alarm
GRIMACE	A twisting of the face that expresses pain, contempt, or disgust
HEEDLESS	Not paying attention
HOVER	Hang about; wait nearby

HUMILIATING	Lowering the pride, dignity, or self-respect
IMPERIAL	Having supreme authority
INCREDULITY	Disbelief
INSIDIOUS	Intended to entrap; treacherous
LACKEYS	Slaves; forced laborers
LOATHING	Great dislike; abhorrence

MERIDIAN	Highest point; peak
MERITORIOUS	Deserving reward or praise
MIASMAS	Swamp gas; odor of decaying matter
MOLEST	To disturb, interfere with, or annoy
ODIOUS	Arousing strong dislike or intense displeasure
OMINOUS	Threatening

OSTENTATION	Boastful display meant to impress others; showiness
PALLID	Having an abnormally pale complexion
PESTILENCE	A destructive, evil influence
PRECEPTS	Rules or principles
PRESUMPTUOUS	Going beyond what is right or proper; excessively forward
PUNGENCY	Stinging; capable of burning

PURGING	Purifying; cleansing
REMONSTRATING	Pleading in protest
REMUNERATION	Payment
SAPLING	A young tree
SEINE	Net for catching fish
SINISTER	Evil

SOLACE	Comfort in trouble
SOMBER	Dark; gloomy
STEALTHY	Acting with secrecy to avoid notice
STOLID	Having or revealing little emotion
SUBJUGATION	Act of bringing under control; conquering
SUFFOCATING	Killing by taking away oxygen

SULLEN	Brooding; morose; sulky
TAINTED	Stained; infected; spoiled
TRIBULATIONS	Great afflictions or suffering
TRUSSED	Tied up
VALOR	Courage; bravery
VARMINT	One that is considered undesirable, obnoxious, or troublesome

| VERMILION | A vivid red to reddish orange |
| VOLITION | A conscious choice or decision |

Light in the Forest Vocabulary

TRIBULATIONS	MERIDIAN	AVERSION	DEBASED	VARMINT
SOMBER	PURGING	SULLEN	VOLITION	ABDUCTOR
DISPOSITION	HUMILIATING	FREE SPACE	COUNSEL	FILIAL
CONDONE	SUFFOCATING	OMINOUS	DESTINATION	GRIMACE
PRECEPTS	SINISTER	ODIOUS	EXERTION	INSIDIOUS

Light in the Forest Vocabulary

OSTENTATION	FATHOM	EXEMPLARY	STOLID	DOUGHTIER
VERMILION	REMONSTRATING	LACKEYS	ALOOFNESS	PESTILENCE
PALLID	STEALTHY	FREE SPACE	MOLEST	ENDURE
DERISION	SOLACE	TRUSSED	DISCERNED	DETERRED
MIASMAS	DESOLATE	SUBJUGATION	APPEASE	INCREDULITY

Light in the Forest Vocabulary

DISTORTED	PRECEPTS	SEINE	STOLID	ALOOFNESS
LOATHING	VALOR	PESTILENCE	BLEAKLY	MERIDIAN
FATHOM	STEALTHY	FREE SPACE	ALACRITY	CONDONE
AVERSION	SINISTER	ALLOTTED	SAPLING	SUFFOCATING
DISPOSITION	DESOLATE	MERITORIOUS	DESTINATION	BERATING

Light in the Forest Vocabulary

FILIAL	MIASMAS	VOLITION	FORMIDABLE	PALLID
TAINTED	DEFIANT	COVET	INCREDULITY	ABDUCTOR
DERISION	MOLEST	FREE SPACE	REMONSTRATING	SOMBER
TRUSSED	ASSENTED	DISCERNED	SULLEN	INSIDIOUS
GRIMACE	REMUNERATION	OMINOUS	HEEDLESS	HOVER

Light in the Forest Vocabulary

PRESUMPTUOUS	DESOLATE	VARMINT	SEINE	COUNSEL
ALACRITY	DISCERNED	ABDUCTOR	INSIDIOUS	STEALTHY
TRIBULATIONS	EXULTATION	FREE SPACE	MOLEST	ALLOTTED
ABHORRENCE	HUMILIATING	BERATING	DOUGHTIER	SULLEN
VALOR	TAINTED	DEFIANT	PESTILENCE	DERISION

Light in the Forest Vocabulary

SAPLING	REMUNERATION	DISTORTED	AVERSION	SINISTER
ENCUMBRANCES	ALOOFNESS	MERIDIAN	BUSTLE	ENDURE
ASSENTED	SUFFOCATING	FREE SPACE	OSTENTATION	FILIAL
PUNGENCY	LOATHING	DETERRED	VOLITION	EXEMPLARY
ODIOUS	REMONSTRATING	STOLID	DEBASED	BLEAKLY

Light in the Forest Vocabulary

PESTILENCE	ALLOTTED	MIASMAS	HEEDLESS	HUMILIATING
MERITORIOUS	INCREDULITY	PUNGENCY	FILIAL	SOMBER
ABHORRENCE	EXEMPLARY	FREE SPACE	HOVER	VALOR
SOLACE	REMONSTRATING	BUSTLE	OMINOUS	VERMILION
TRUSSED	DEBASED	DEFIANT	OSTENTATION	DISTORTED

Light in the Forest Vocabulary

FORMIDABLE	DERISION	ABDUCTOR	ASSENTED	MOLEST
ALACRITY	STOLID	FATHOM	DISPOSITION	INSIDIOUS
BLEAKLY	ENCUMBRANCES	FREE SPACE	DOUGHTIER	BERATING
DESTINATION	ALOOFNESS	CONSOLATION	MERIDIAN	PRECEPTS
EXULTATION	SUBJUGATION	SEINE	SINISTER	STEALTHY

Light in the Forest Vocabulary

PRECEPTS	LACKEYS	REMONSTRATING	OMINOUS	HUMILIATING
ALOOFNESS	SEINE	BERATING	CONDONE	MIASMAS
CONSOLATION	IMPERIAL	FREE SPACE	DEFIANT	LOATHING
STOLID	DESOLATE	PUNGENCY	ODIOUS	HOVER
ALLOTTED	VARMINT	MERITORIOUS	DESTINATION	DETERRED

Light in the Forest Vocabulary

TRIBULATIONS	SOLACE	DEBASED	FILIAL	FORMIDABLE
PURGING	DISPOSITION	BUSTLE	COVET	SUBJUGATION
SUFFOCATING	DISCERNED	FREE SPACE	SULLEN	ALACRITY
DISTORTED	SAPLING	COUNSEL	OSTENTATION	ENDURE
DERISION	ABHORRENCE	HEEDLESS	DOUGHTIER	VOLITION

Light in the Forest Vocabulary

HEEDLESS	PALLID	HUMILIATING	INSIDIOUS	DISCERNED
BLEAKLY	DISTORTED	GRIMACE	ODIOUS	DESOLATE
PURGING	SULLEN	FREE SPACE	OSTENTATION	SUFFOCATING
CONDONE	DISPOSITION	STEALTHY	BUSTLE	INCREDULITY
MOLEST	DOUGHTIER	TRIBULATIONS	TAINTED	DEFIANT

Light in the Forest Vocabulary

APPEASE	PUNGENCY	SOMBER	TRUSSED	BERATING
PESTILENCE	DERISION	MERITORIOUS	OMINOUS	DESTINATION
SOLACE	FILIAL	FREE SPACE	PRESUMPTUOUS	AVERSION
SUBJUGATION	ALACRITY	PRECEPTS	SINISTER	LACKEYS
DETERRED	REMUNERATION	MERIDIAN	VERMILION	SAPLING

Light in the Forest Vocabulary

ABHORRENCE	LOATHING	CONDONE	COUNSEL	SOLACE
DOUGHTIER	SUBJUGATION	ASSENTED	OSTENTATION	INSIDIOUS
BLEAKLY	EXEMPLARY	FREE SPACE	DESTINATION	DEFIANT
COVET	FORMIDABLE	TAINTED	STEALTHY	HEEDLESS
VOLITION	ENDURE	PESTILENCE	SINISTER	REMUNERATION

Light in the Forest Vocabulary

BUSTLE	OMINOUS	IMPERIAL	SAPLING	PURGING
ENCUMBRANCES	DISCERNED	EXULTATION	SUFFOCATING	DESOLATE
ODIOUS	BERATING	FREE SPACE	VERMILION	DERISION
STOLID	MIASMAS	PALLID	DETERRED	TRIBULATIONS
TRUSSED	FATHOM	AVERSION	INCREDULITY	SEINE

Light in the Forest Vocabulary

SINISTER	VERMILION	REMUNERATION	HOVER	INCREDULITY
SUBJUGATION	FATHOM	ENDURE	TRIBULATIONS	PURGING
SULLEN	PRESUMPTUOUS	FREE SPACE	VARMINT	DEFIANT
SOMBER	ENCUMBRANCES	ASSENTED	MOLEST	EXEMPLARY
DISTORTED	PRECEPTS	DERISION	ALLOTTED	BUSTLE

Light in the Forest Vocabulary

ALACRITY	REMONSTRATING	SEINE	GRIMACE	EXULTATION
ODIOUS	OMINOUS	MIASMAS	OSTENTATION	INSIDIOUS
FORMIDABLE	HUMILIATING	FREE SPACE	APPEASE	MERITORIOUS
PALLID	PESTILENCE	COUNSEL	BERATING	IMPERIAL
SOLACE	ALOOFNESS	HEEDLESS	ABDUCTOR	DISPOSITION

Light in the Forest Vocabulary

VERMILION	LACKEYS	PRECEPTS	EXULTATION	SEINE
DOUGHTIER	STEALTHY	SUFFOCATING	ODIOUS	REMUNERATION
DEBASED	DEFIANT	FREE SPACE	HEEDLESS	TAINTED
INCREDULITY	MOLEST	ALACRITY	BERATING	CONSOLATION
COVET	BLEAKLY	DETERRED	SAPLING	ABDUCTOR

Light in the Forest Vocabulary

BUSTLE	MERIDIAN	AVERSION	EXERTION	REMONSTRATING
STOLID	PESTILENCE	FATHOM	CONDONE	LOATHING
OMINOUS	IMPERIAL	FREE SPACE	SUBJUGATION	OSTENTATION
PUNGENCY	GRIMACE	ENCUMBRANCES	DISCERNED	VARMINT
MERITORIOUS	HUMILIATING	DISTORTED	SINISTER	VALOR

Light in the Forest Vocabulary

BERATING	AVERSION	ODIOUS	VOLITION	PRECEPTS
SINISTER	OSTENTATION	LOATHING	STEALTHY	ENCUMBRANCES
SOLACE	ALOOFNESS	FREE SPACE	LACKEYS	ALACRITY
FILIAL	PESTILENCE	INCREDULITY	CONDONE	MERIDIAN
OMINOUS	FATHOM	COVET	DERISION	PALLID

Light in the Forest Vocabulary

INSIDIOUS	ABDUCTOR	TRIBULATIONS	EXULTATION	DEBASED
SAPLING	VALOR	PUNGENCY	HUMILIATING	SOMBER
IMPERIAL	CONSOLATION	FREE SPACE	HOVER	DISTORTED
MERITORIOUS	PURGING	FORMIDABLE	ALLOTTED	TRUSSED
DISCERNED	VERMILION	REMUNERATION	ENDURE	COUNSEL

Light in the Forest Vocabulary

ENDURE	ODIOUS	LACKEYS	VERMILION	DERISION
STEALTHY	BLEAKLY	DESTINATION	EXEMPLARY	VOLITION
BERATING	DEBASED	FREE SPACE	SULLEN	DOUGHTIER
INSIDIOUS	ASSENTED	HUMILIATING	PALLID	VARMINT
SINISTER	COUNSEL	MOLEST	SOMBER	INCREDULITY

Light in the Forest Vocabulary

COVET	ALLOTTED	SOLACE	PRECEPTS	OMINOUS
AVERSION	PRESUMPTUOUS	TRIBULATIONS	STOLID	DESOLATE
GRIMACE	OSTENTATION	FREE SPACE	MERIDIAN	FORMIDABLE
SUBJUGATION	APPEASE	ABHORRENCE	ABDUCTOR	DISPOSITION
HOVER	MERITORIOUS	TAINTED	LOATHING	ALOOFNESS

Light in the Forest Vocabulary

SUBJUGATION	BERATING	INCREDULITY	DESOLATE	HOVER
SAPLING	REMUNERATION	BUSTLE	PUNGENCY	SUFFOCATING
HEEDLESS	OMINOUS	FREE SPACE	EXULTATION	APPEASE
MOLEST	LACKEYS	SULLEN	FATHOM	SINISTER
EXERTION	DETERRED	ODIOUS	MERIDIAN	REMONSTRATING

Light in the Forest Vocabulary

ASSENTED	PRECEPTS	VERMILION	DERISION	CONDONE
SOMBER	FILIAL	PURGING	PALLID	AVERSION
GRIMACE	STEALTHY	FREE SPACE	IMPERIAL	COVET
DEBASED	TRIBULATIONS	DISCERNED	PRESUMPTUOUS	MIASMAS
STOLID	ABHORRENCE	FORMIDABLE	BLEAKLY	COUNSEL

Light in the Forest Vocabulary

COVET	TAINTED	FORMIDABLE	MERIDIAN	LOATHING
CONSOLATION	REMONSTRATING	SOMBER	APPEASE	DISTORTED
EXERTION	IMPERIAL	FREE SPACE	VARMINT	SUFFOCATING
DETERRED	PUNGENCY	PRECEPTS	COUNSEL	LACKEYS
SINISTER	EXEMPLARY	ALLOTTED	VOLITION	SULLEN

Light in the Forest Vocabulary

DERISION	SOLACE	HOVER	FATHOM	OMINOUS
DEFIANT	ABDUCTOR	MOLEST	ALOOFNESS	REMUNERATION
PESTILENCE	BUSTLE	FREE SPACE	DISCERNED	STOLID
INSIDIOUS	ASSENTED	PURGING	AVERSION	HUMILIATING
HEEDLESS	TRIBULATIONS	ENDURE	MIASMAS	FILIAL

Light in the Forest Vocabulary

BERATING	OMINOUS	ABHORRENCE	BUSTLE	EXULTATION
OSTENTATION	PALLID	FORMIDABLE	TAINTED	ABDUCTOR
DESTINATION	HOVER	FREE SPACE	COUNSEL	MIASMAS
SEINE	PURGING	EXEMPLARY	DEBASED	CONDONE
SINISTER	SOMBER	VERMILION	ALLOTTED	MERIDIAN

Light in the Forest Vocabulary

HEEDLESS	ALACRITY	REMONSTRATING	IMPERIAL	AVERSION
INSIDIOUS	APPEASE	DETERRED	DISCERNED	SOLACE
REMUNERATION	SAPLING	FREE SPACE	FILIAL	ASSENTED
DESOLATE	CONSOLATION	DEFIANT	PRECEPTS	VALOR
DOUGHTIER	VARMINT	TRUSSED	LOATHING	COVET

Light in the Forest Vocabulary

PUNGENCY	SOMBER	PRECEPTS	DEBASED	ABHORRENCE
DISPOSITION	DESOLATE	IMPERIAL	EXULTATION	PESTILENCE
EXEMPLARY	ALLOTTED	FREE SPACE	HOVER	TRIBULATIONS
DISTORTED	SEINE	MERITORIOUS	VARMINT	ALOOFNESS
BLEAKLY	GRIMACE	VOLITION	DEFIANT	ASSENTED

Light in the Forest Vocabulary

STEALTHY	OMINOUS	VALOR	DESTINATION	BERATING
SUFFOCATING	VERMILION	DERISION	LOATHING	TRUSSED
AVERSION	SOLACE	FREE SPACE	DETERRED	OSTENTATION
LACKEYS	DOUGHTIER	DISCERNED	SUBJUGATION	COVET
STOLID	MIASMAS	COUNSEL	REMUNERATION	ENDURE

Light in the Forest Vocabulary

COUNSEL	SEINE	ALACRITY	SINISTER	DEBASED
BLEAKLY	ENCUMBRANCES	MOLEST	ALLOTTED	FORMIDABLE
LOATHING	DETERRED	FREE SPACE	HUMILIATING	DEFIANT
SULLEN	DISTORTED	INCREDULITY	FILIAL	VARMINT
HOVER	REMUNERATION	TRUSSED	ODIOUS	ASSENTED

Light in the Forest Vocabulary

SOLACE	AVERSION	APPEASE	STEALTHY	SUBJUGATION
PALLID	BERATING	GRIMACE	PURGING	LACKEYS
COVET	MIASMAS	FREE SPACE	VOLITION	ABDUCTOR
EXERTION	DISPOSITION	VERMILION	SUFFOCATING	PESTILENCE
DERISION	IMPERIAL	BUSTLE	OMINOUS	ALOOFNESS

www.ingramcontent.com/pod-product-compliance
Lightning Source LLC
Chambersburg PA
CBHW081453070526
44586CB00019B/2330